The Cuban
Revolution
into the 1990s

Latin American Perspectives Series

Ronald H. Chilcote, Series Editor

† Available in hardcover and paperback.

The Cuban Revolution into the 1990s

Cuban Perspectives

edited by
Centro de Estudios
Sobre América

Westview Press
Boulder • San Francisco • Oxford

Latin American Perspective Series, Number 10

Published in 1992 in the United States of America by Westview Press, Inc., 5500 Central Avenue, Boulder, Colorado 80301-2877, and in the United Kingdom by Westview Press, 36 Lonsdale Road, Summertown, Oxford OX2 7EW

Library of Congress Cataloging-in-Publication Data
The Cuban Revolution into the 1990s: Cuban perspectives / edited by
Centro de Estudios Sobre América.
    p.   cm. — (Latin American perspectives series ; no. 10)
    Includes bibliographical references and index.
    ISBN 0-8133-1186-1. — ISBN 0-8133-1187-X (pbk.)
    1. Cuba—Politics and government—1959– 2. Cuba—Economic
conditions—1959– 3. Cuba—Social conditions—1959– I. Centro de
Estudios Sobre América. II. Series.
F1788.C829   1992
972.9106′4—dc20   92-14477
                                                                            CIP

Printed and bound in the United States of America

∞ The paper used in this publication meets the requirements
of the American National Standard for Permanence of Paper
for Printed Library Materials Z39.48-1984.

10   9   8   7   6   5   4   3   2   1

Contents

Introduction

Ronald H. Chilcote

The Cuban Revolution succeeded in 1959 in the face of official U.S. opposition, an abortive Bay of Pigs invasion, and an economic embargo. Cuban dependence on the United States dated to the U.S. occupation of the island from 1898 to 1901 and subsequent interventions in 1906–1909, 1912, and 1917. Historically, the Cuban economy has depended on the export of sugar. Before the revolution the United States imported the largest share of Cuban sugar; after 1960 the Soviet Union assumed this role, and in exchange Cuba had to import its fuel and some of its foodstuffs, raw materials, and capital goods.

Early efforts at central planning in a previously undisciplined economic system encountered many problems. Foreign exchange reserves declined, and raw materials for new factories had to be imported at prices exceeding the cost of importing many finished goods. The goal of producing 1 million tons of sugar in 1970 was not achieved. There were, however, some advances, including new technology for sugarcane production and the commercialization of many by-products, diversification into other agricultural products, crossbreeding to produce cattle both resistant to the tropical climate and capable of producing greater quantities of milk, and expansion and modernization of the fishing industry. According to Andrew Zimbalist, from 1960 to 1985 Cuba outperformed the rest of Latin America, with real

Ronald H. Chilcote is professor of political science and economics at the University of California, Riverside, and managing editor of *Latin American Perspectives* and, with Sheryl Lutjens, an editor and compiler of *Cuba, 1953–1978: A Bibliographical Guide to the Literature* (1986).

per capita income increasing an average of 3 percent compared with less than 2 percent, a substantially more equitable distribution of income, and unemployment well below the Latin American average (*Multinational Monitor*, April 1989). The revolution's objective of providing all Cubans with free services in areas of basic needs such as health, education, welfare, and housing led to spectacular advances in health care (in particular, an integrated system of prevention and treatment) and in nutrition, water, and sewage disposal, the reduction of illiteracy to less than 4 percent of the population, and the construction of new housing that, however, failed to keep pace with the demand created by concentration in certain areas and population growth. Politics revolved around the charismatic personality of Fidel Castro, who had led the abortive assault on the Moncada barracks in 1953 and the guerrilla struggle later in the decade. The Partido Comunista de Cuba (Communist Party of Cuba, PCC) dominated political life at the top, but other political institutions were also important: Poder Popular (People's Power), a system of elected people's assemblies at the municipal, provincial, and national levels; local Comités de Defensa de la Revolución (Committees for the Defense of the Revolution, CDRs), charged with guarding against counterrevolutionary activities and serving neighborhood needs; and popular courts (*tribunales populares*) to deal with disputes and petty crimes at the neighborhood level.

In 1989, as the Berlin Wall crumbled, the command socialist economies of Eastern Europe began to collapse one after another, and the Soviet Union moved toward a market economy, the Cuban economy was confronted with serious problems. The reduction of Soviet petroleum deliveries by 25 percent led to an energy crisis and the loss of a surplus normally reexported for needed hard currency. The unification of Germany deprived Cuba of its second-largest trading partner. Its foreign commerce was further undermined by the abandonment of the system of barter and preferential prices maintained by the Soviet Union and its former Eastern European partners and by the need to trade in hard (dollar) currency. Under the trade agreement with Moscow signed in December 1990, Cuba would pay more for Soviet petroleum and receive less for sugar, assume some of the shipping costs formerly absorbed by Moscow, and lose the services of a thousand Soviet technicians.

In an attempt to accommodate both the U.S. embargo and the changing Soviet relations, Cuba embarked on an emergency program of energy reduction and food rationing. While Cubans had long ago learned to deal with shortages and make sacrifices, the crisis necessitated new thinking, the raising of new questions, and the reworking of old ideas in creative and refreshing ways. Cuban intellectuals and academicians are today undertaking these tasks. Their work suffered in the early years both from the amount of effort required to accomplish the goals of the revolution and from problems characteristic of the Third World such as poor training and lack of skills, shortage of resources, and limited attention to scholarship outside priority areas. Moreover, the threat of U.S. imperialism meant that they worked in an atmosphere of vigilance against counterrevolutionary activities, a controlled press, and constraints on political activity. Although the quality of academic work has gradually improved over the years, scholarship has necessarily focused on policy questions as intellectuals assess successes and failures and search for a better society in the face of the seemingly insatiable demands of the international capitalist order. This volume brings together some of their perspectives on issues that include not only economic adjustments but the expansion of political opportunities, the enhancement of the notable social advances of the revolution, and the identification of a role for the highly educated and skilled younger generation that will eventually assume positions of responsibility.

Organized around the themes of democracy and socialism, economic development, and social issues in contemporary Cuba, the chapters offer retrospective views of the Cuban Revolution, its origins, and the difficulties in its evolution to the present day. They anticipate questions related to the difficult path ahead as Cuba prepares to confront changing trade relations and diminishing aid from its traditional sources, a large external debt, and domestic shortages in material goods. Finally, they emphasize the accomplishments of the past thirty years, especially in health care, education, and social services and in economic development and infrastructure.

Questions of democracy and socialism are the focus of Part One. The Cuban agenda has long included attention to the building of democracy, and democracy has usually been identifiable through the institutions mentioned above even though the Party, wary of U.S. interference and counterrevolutionary activities, has controlled political opportunity through a restricted press and other means. This control emerged as an issue in debates at the Party's fourth congress in October 1991, although few substantive changes were ultimately approved. Julio Carranza Valdés argues here that the process of rectification begun in 1986 represents an opportunity to revise and correct errors and negative tendencies in contemporary Cuba. He candidly alludes to the squandering of scarce resources, excessive individual material interest, corruption, and undemocratic behavior, but he also identifies ways in which Cuba has confronted these and other problems. He examines redistribution of income as a measure of democracy in the economy and associates the guarantee of certain social services with social equality. He argues that the single party and the political system evolved through a complicated historical process that differed from that in both Eastern Europe and the Third World and, while acknowledging restrictions on democratic liberties, past and present, holds that the contradictions and tensions today relate to the need for more political space "through the revolution, not outside of it."

Juan Antonio Blanco takes as his point of departure the premises that the Cuban Revolution is a historical *process*, that it must be examined in its national and international context, and that it has its own logic and rationality. Assessing its achievements after thirty years, he argues that socialism in Cuba was not the consequence of a prescribed course but evolved through a classist option for defending socialist development in the face of a hostile foreign power. Pointing to the lessons that can be learned from Cuba's experiments with participatory democracy, he contrasts this experience with the limitations of representative democracy in the United States and elsewhere. Cuba's problems, he argues, are the consequence of both U.S. pressure and conceptual errors, and its revolutionary process must continue to develop in its own creative and unique way.

Rafael Hernández and Haroldo Dilla apply the concept of political culture to an assessment of the participation of the citizenry in Cuban life. They argue that the Cuban Revolution transformed Cuban culture, national values, and ideology. Their provocative essay explores the basis and extent of participation through an examination of key historical moments in the Cuban experience.

Georgina Suárez Hernández examines the new political leadership after 1959, focusing on the institutionalization process and the means whereby these leaders were able to mobilize the population for effective participation in society. Her discussion distinguishes an initial stage in the evolution of the new leadership from a later one that began with the implementation of Poder Popular and efforts to expand democratic participation. She cautiously approaches the question of democracy within a single party and the need to reevaluate participation in the present stage of the revolution.

Fernando Martínez Heredia turns to criticisms raised in the course of the rectification process and argues that Cuban socialism has evolved from the struggle to free the country from foreign domination and to ensure sovereignty and self-determination, the mobilization of popular forces, the reorganization of production, and the expansion of political participation. He briefly assesses Cuba's accomplishments, differentiating its socialism from the experience in Eastern Europe. He argues that Cuba must adhere to its principles while remaining flexible in dealing with the broad range of interests that shape social progress and confronting the tensions among interest groups within the country and the demands of the international situation.

Finally, Armando Hart Dávalos examines the lessons of Che Guevara's work in the present context. He reminds us that Che supported methods of economic management and control that had evolved in the historical experience of capitalism. He urges a return to this and other ideas Che raised a quarter-century ago as one means of searching for practical and concrete solutions to Cuban problems today.

Part Two consists of four chapters by prominent Cuban economists. Carlos Tablada shows that Che Guevara's proposals for central planning were premised on the application to the Cuban revolutionary process of modifications and adaptations of advanced capitalist technology and organization. He argues that the ongoing process of rectification involves an assessment of current problems, corruption, and mismanagement through a reevaluation of Guevara's thought. José Luis Rodríguez García examines changes in the economy over the past thirty years and the impact on it of the rectification process. Miguel Alejandro Figueras looks at the structural changes implemented by the revolution, the problems that arose during the 1970s, and the reorganization during the ensuing decade that brought an increase in production for export beyond the traditional sugar sector. He goes on to subject that sector to detailed historical analysis.

Part Three deals with social questions. In a brief piece on an important theme on which there is a dearth of scholarship, Juan Luis Martín reveals that two-fifths of the country's professionals and technicians are between seventeen and twenty-nine years of age. He analyzes the important problems facing the younger generation and the issue of employment for the highly skilled and professional labor force. Although this generation has had no direct contact with the insurgency and the early years of the revolution, he points out, it will soon take the place of the founding generation of leaders. Inés Cristina Reca looks at social policy and the family under socialism in Cuba, a subject not significantly dealt with in the scholarly literature. She examines patterns of family relations in a society evolving toward socialism and concludes that while socialist relations serve as a foundation, the socialist family does not necessarily evolve without contradictions or develop in the same way across all classes and social groups. Manuel Limonta Vidal and Guillermo Padrón look at the surprising development of biotechnology and its medical applications in Cuba, pointing to the resources that have been invested in transplant surgery, on the one hand, and in new technologies, on the other, and describing advances in work on interferon, treatments for burn patients, and new approaches to diseases such as AIDS and leprosy. On another relatively unknown theme, Raúl Gómez Treto explains how Cuban revolutionary penal law has shaped and adapted to the social and political situation of the country. In particular, he looks at the way in which revolutionary power responded to counterrevolutionary actions and changed when those actions diminished.

The organization of this volume involved the collaboration of the editors of the journal *Latin American Perspectives* in southern California and of scholars at the Centro de Estudios sobre América in Havana. Initially *LAP* intended to publish a volume commemorating the thirtieth anniversary of the Cuban Revolution. Editors Frances Chilcote, Ronald Chilcote, and Richard Harris visited Cuba in 1987 and 1988 in search of publishable material. Some forty essays presented by Cubans at the international conference "30 Years of the Cuban Revolution" in Halifax in early November 1989 also yielded some interesting material. The editors evaluated all the available essays in December 1989, recommended decisions and revisions, and sent a report and reviews to Cuban authors. Three editors (Marjorie Bray, Ronald Chilcote, and Jennifer Dugan Abbassi) visited Havana in March and April 1990 to work with authors and facilitate revisions as well as find additional manuscripts. Rafael Hernández coordinated these activities and encouraged Cuban authors to submit final drafts by summer 1990. *LAP* assumed the responsibility for organizing a team of translators, and Westview Press advanced funds to help with this task. We are especially grateful to Jennifer Dugan Abbassi, Diana Alarcón, James Bloyd, Jean Díaz, Margaret Gilpin, Terry McKinley, Phil Martínez, Janell Pierce, Sarah Stookey, Clare Weber, and Aníbal Yáñez for committing themselves to the project as translators and meeting deadlines. We thank those who worked carefully with the translators to edit their work and insist in revision, including Jennifer Dugan Abbassi, Marjorie Bray, Frances Chilcote, Timothy Harding, Barbara Metzger, Marina Pianca, and Sarah Stookey. Barbara Ellington of Westview Press was especially encouraging and helpful with queries and suggestions for further revision, and Jennifer Dugan Abbassi assisted in this revision and also prepared the index.

We are appreciative of Sage Publications' permission to publish essays by Julio Carranza Valdés, Fernando Martínez Heredia, Rafael Hernández, Haroldo Dilla, Georgina Suárez Hernández, Miguel Alejandro Figueras, Juan Luis Martín, Manuel Limonta Vidal, Guillermo Padrón, and Raúl Gómez Treto that appeared, in most cases in different form, in *Latin American Perspectives* 18 (Spring 1991). We are grateful to Pathfinder Press for permission to publish the essay by Carlos Tablada, which appeared in a different and fuller version in *New International* 9 (1991). Finally, the organizers of the Halifax conference would like to acknowledge the generous support of the following sponsors: the Ford Foundation, the MacArthur Foundation, Saint Mary's University, the International Education Centre, Dalhousie University, the Lester Pearson Institute, Mount

St. Vincent University, and the Canadian Association for Latin American and Caribbean Studies.

This volume complements another one in Westview's Latin American Perspectives series entitled *Cuba in Transition: Crisis and Transformation* and edited by Sandor Halebsky, John M. Kirk, Carolee Bengelsdorf, Richard Harris, Jean Stubbes, and Andrew Zimbalist. Readers are encouraged to compare these analyses by Cuban scholars with those of established scholars of Cuba residing elsewhere.

PART 1
Democracy and Socialism

1

Reform and the Future of Cuban Socialism

Julio Carranza Valdés

Translated by Clare Weber

One of the most worrisome issues in Cuba today is the impact of the changes taking place in socialist Europe. I will try to give an overview of the situation and offer some personal reflections.

When we examine the historical development of the Cuban Revolution, we can identify various moments of critical reflection on it and assessment of what remains to be done. The process of rectification initiated in 1986 is only one of these, and it will probably not be the last. It is an error to believe that this process is a consequence of *perestroika* and the changes occurring in socialist Europe; in fact it preceded those changes.

A very serious crisis of foreign exchange reserves in 1985 led to an urgent pursuit of renegotiation of the debt with member countries of the Paris Club. Although some agreements were reached, they were insufficient to resolve the crisis. The resulting tensions within the economy led to a set of measures to increase the availability of foreign exchange: the production of exportable goods for favorable placement in the international market, the reduction of imports, and an increase in efficiency in the internal economy. At this point one began to see failures in the planning and management of the economy that created new social and political problems.

Because of inefficiencies and other problems, scarce resources were squandered. Bureaucratism flourished, and, increasingly, payment was exacted for services not performed (for example, a business theoretically dedicated to the painting of buildings would simply sell paint to consumers instead of performing the actual painting service itself, although the cost of this service would be included in the price). Beyond this, there was excessive individual material interest, inordinate privatization of certain services, a predominance of undemocratic points of view, the use of positions to obtain privileges and material advantages, corruption, mockery of the legal and economic order by enterprises and organizations, lack of incentive, uncritical pursuit of other socialist experiments, and an impoverishment of political-ideological work.

The objective of the process of rectification is the resolution of these and other negative tendencies. This process has already produced an evaluation of the system of administration and planning of the economy initiated in 1975, the year of the first Party congress—a new chapter of a discussion that has been going on in Cuba since the 1960s. Today there is consensus within the country on the existence of these deviations and errors in the Cuban economy; the debate is associated with attempting to identify their causes.

The situation in Cuba has also produced a profound rethinking of the revolutionary experience in all sectors of society. On this there have been contradictory positions, ranging from that which regards the system of self-financing adopted in 1975 as contrary to the strategic interests of socialism to that which considers the system fundamentally correct but its implementation incomplete, inconsistent, and incoherent. Advocates of the latter see a solution in the revision and improvement of the system already established. In view of the complexity of the situation, the immediate decision has been to take time to discuss these aspects in depth and develop some experiments in certain enterprises. The resultant experiences will be incorporated into the debate that leads to the ultimate decisions on the most important issues.

A central point of all this discussion regards the political work required by a prerevolutionary process like that taking place in Cuba, an underdeveloped country located in an area of geopolitical interest to the United States, and the relation of that work to the operation of certain market mechanisms. Although the discussion is still in progress, the tendency has been to seek a balance that recognizes the role of economic stimulation and the solution of individual material problems as an important lever for development but also recovers the fundamental role of political work— construction of a social consciousness that guarantees the commitment of the majority to the objectives of the project and to the sacrifices that inevitably must be made to achieve it.

While these questions of direction and planning of the economy are being debated, measures have had to be taken to deal with a series of social problems whose solution the masses were strongly demanding. These measures have had to do with such programs as the construction of housing and of schools for the handicapped, the reconstruction of schools in the provinces, and the expansion of the health care system, which, although already operating at an impressive level, was insufficient to meet the demand. New hospitals have been built and many of the existing ones expanded. In addition, centers have been established throughout the country where resident doctors and nurses provide medical attention to the approximately 120 families of each barrio. Because the incorporation of a large part of the female work force into the workplace had been delayed by the scarcity of infant and child care centers, 54 such centers were constructed in one year in the city of Havana alone. Finally, new food programs have been developed to guarantee the population a substantial increase in basic foodstuffs.

At the same time, a set of strategic investments has been made for the development of export industries, for import substitution, and for the development of the tourist infrastructure as alternative sources of profits and foreign exchange for the future. There has also been an important move toward what we call "leading sectors"—research on and production of the products of the biotechnological and pharmaceutical industries, both of which are reaching important export levels. In 1989, the export of antimeningitis vaccine was one of the greatest earners of foreign exchange. All of this has been accompanied by the introduction of new forms of organization of the work force such as microbrigades and "contingents" that are expected to bring a higher level of efficiency. These efforts and the continuing debate on the organizational forms to be adopted in the economy and the society are taking place in the midst of financial pressures and the reinforcement of the North American blockade. The transformation of socialist Europe places additional pressure on the process of change.

In order to cope with the crises in the international economy, in 1985 Cuba reduced its commercial and financial relations with the West to a mere 13.8 percent, which meant that its trade and financial exchange with socialist Europe reached 86.2 percent of all its external economic relations. These proportions convey some idea of the strong impact on the Cuban economy of the changes in the economies of the socialist countries. Cancellations, modifications, and delays in previous agreements came from many of the governmental enterprises of socialist Europe. The Soviet government often expressed its willingness to maintain the historically supportive relations between the two countries. Nevertheless, and independent of this, the role granted to enterprises in the economic reorganization of the Soviet Union and the other socialist countries impacted external economic relations. This impact forced a redefinition of Cuba's participation in the world market and an attempt to reinvigorate the internal economy.

In 1988 Hungary was to have sent Cuba an important cargo of transmissions and engines for the construction of buses that would provide urban transportation in the major cities of the country. These shipments were delayed and when they arrived were incomplete because Hungarian enterprises found the world market a much more profitable place to sell products than Cuba. This situation resulted in a great shortage of replacement parts and caused serious problems for Cuban urban transportation. Beyond the economic implications there were political ones that resulted from public discomfort and dissatisfaction. The only viable course was to develop the production of transmissions and engines in Cuba, and a year and a half later the first Cuban transmissions and engines were in use.

The fundamental principle of all these adjustments has been to affect as little as possible the standard of living of the majority of the people and to maintain the principal social achievements of the revolution. During the past six years, in spite of the precariousness of resources, expenditures on social security and assistance (the first cuts that a country with these tensions would normally make) increased by 36.01 percent. Spending on education and health increased 45.5 percent and on sociocultural activities and scientific development 49.4 percent.

The accepted definition of democracy is equality plus participation—the involvement of the majority in discussion, decision making, and the implementation of the decisions that have been made. From this point of view, the Cuban Revolution has also been a process of democratic construction. In the first place, its redistribution of income has permitted the achievement of important levels of social equality. We see this achievement in the development of radical agrarian reform, urban reform, the nationalization of foreign-owned properties, the privatization of medium-sized and large enterprises, the system of social security, education, and free health care, and so on. Obviously, however, to reduce democratic practice to certain achievements in the economic field would be to impoverish the very concept of democracy. Democracy is incomplete if social equality is not accompanied by the participation of the majority in decisions on matters that affect their lives.

On a second level, therefore, is the construction of a political system that guarantees the participation of the majority, and here it is important that the existence of a single party in Cuba is not the result of any ideological conception but the outcome of a complicated historical process different from those that developed in Eastern Europe, Africa, and Central America. The bourgeois political parties of the opposition did not participate in the fight against the dictator, not even at the moment of revolutionary triumph: They went to Miami. Three parties of the left were able, in a complicated process, to agree to merge into a single party constructed not upon any philosophical-political doctrine but upon a concrete revolutionary program that responded to concrete Cuban problems. The result was the union in 1965–1967 of the Directorio Revolucionario (Revolutionary Directorate), the Movimiento 26 de Julio (26th of July Movement), and the Partido Socialista Popular (People's Socialist Party) in the Partido Comunista de Cuba. Parallel to this party, the result of a historical process, there developed a number of mass organizations based upon popular participation: the Comités de Defensa de la Revolución, the Federación de Mujeres Cubanas (Federation of Cuban Women), the student federations, the associations of farmers, artisans, economists, doctors, lawyers, architects, and so on, the Central de Trabajadores de Cuba (Cuban Workers' Federation), with its various unions, and the organs of popular power called Poder Popular. When they were set up they were submitted to a national plebiscite and were approved by an absolute majority.

In this process there have, of course, been restrictions of certain democratic liberties arising from the logic of a process that affected powerful interests in a country that had been dominated by the United States. To have made room, in the first years of the revolution, for interests that were in Miami and meant very little to the people would have reduced the rhythm of the revolution. Obviously, thirty-one years later the question of democracy has other components. Although the institutional apparatus that ought to guarantee broad popular participation has been created and is functioning, it is far from operating as it should. The revelations of corruption of the summer of 1989 unveiled a serious failure of the mechanisms of popular control whose effective functioning should be a fundamental component of democratic participation.

Discussions such as these, with a strong critical component, result in a demand for better performance on the part of the various institutions of power and popular control. Calls for the creation of other institutions or parties are heard only in Miami or in tiny, marginal sectors of Cuban society. The contradictions and fundamental revindications for the masses in Cuba today have to do with errors that have been committed in the Cuban revolutionary process. These differ from those committed in other socialist experiments just as does the context in which our revolution has developed. It would be false to assert that Cuba has no problems and tensions, but it is also an error to consider these problems and tensions the same as those that have been revealed in socialist Europe. The contradictions, tensions, and criticisms existing in Cuba today have to do with the pursuit of more and better spaces within the political system created through the revolution, not outside of it. It is recognized by the majority of the population that the system has permitted the achievement of an objective sought for more than a century: the recovery of the interests of Cuba as a nation.

2

Cuba: Utopia and Reality Thirty Years Later

Juan Antonio Blanco

Translated by James Bloyd

Three decades is not a significant amount of time in historical terms. No historian could have hoped to succeed in arriving at a final verdict on the eighteenth-century French or North American revolutionary process after its first thirty years. Even more difficult would be assessing the vitality and the prospects of a particular social *system* after that much time. It is sufficient to recall that, after its incipient and faltering first steps, European feudalism lasted for centuries and that the general crisis that gradually led to its disappearance spanned a century and a half. This is important to keep in mind if one is to prevent supposedly scientific attempts to evaluate a long-range historical process such as the Cuban Revolution from degenerating into a debate which simply examines part of the historical reality at the expense of others with an eye toward "proving" a political position.

Three decades can, however, be sufficient time for an examination of the correlation between a programmatic project and the practical course of a specific model for the functioning of a social system, which may be useful to the extent that it can be done as "objectively" as is possible for the social scientist ("neutral objectivity" in social research often being not only unattainable but undesirable as well). To establish the conditions for fruitful dialogue, it will therefore be necessary to set forth some methodological precepts:

1. The Cuban Revolution is not a historical *fact* but a historical *process* with profound implications, global and far-reaching in character, that transcend its national scope.
2. Because the context in which the revolution emerges is not propitious for its development free of traumas, detours, and corrections of course, it is essential to measure its results not only in the light of its project but in relation to the national and international environment in which that project has been implemented.
3. To discuss the applicability of the Cuban model to other realities is a mistake; what may be useful is to examine the Cuban option in its most general sense, comparing its current social reality with that of other countries that have pursued development through peripheral-capitalist structures.
4. The functional analysis of the Cuban process must be carried out in terms of its own logic and rationality and keeping in mind that it is unfinished.
5. No human process, however high the ideals that inspire it, is exempt from grave errors, shortcomings, and even excrescences, but the verdict on its course can only be drawn from the historical context in which it develops and is based on its global significance for human progress.

Having established these methodological "rules of the game," we can move on to the key question: Does Cuban praxis up to the present legitimate the historical choice made by the Cuban people thirty years ago?

From the Moncada Program to the Socialist Revolution

In an evaluation of the Cuban Revolution it is pertinent to delineate the political program by which its results are to be measured and, if that original program underwent radical changes, to examine the necessity and legitimacy of those changes. It is therefore necessary to return to the program proposed by the Movimiento 26 de Julio after the assault on the Moncada barracks in 1953, which became the basis for the broad coalition of organizations and sectors of varying ideological and class origins that permitted the overthrow of Fulgencio Batista six years later.

Formally the Moncada Program certainly did not go beyond radical reform, anti-imperialist and popular in nature, within a capitalist legal-structural framework. Respect for private property, generally consecrated by the Constitution of 1940, continued to be indirectly accepted by the program's tacit support of the program of that juridical instrument, and the promised nationalizations were aimed principally at the latifundios and foreign, mostly North American, monopolies. Still, certain projects and laws, such as the one introducing new forms of labor partnership and profit sharing and especially the agrarian reform, showed that the recognition of property rights would not constitute an obstacle to the necessary modification of the way that property was used and to the eventual transformation of its forms and productive employment that would be required for the benefit of the working sectors.

The supposed "change of direction" of the revolution from this *apparently* reformist program (to the extent of its *assertion* that private property would remain the central pillar of its structure) toward a socialist one has long been a subject of debate. There are two principal interpretations of the leadership's intention.

The first claims that the revolution was betrayed—that Fidel Castro and his closest collaborators were already Marxists and never took the Moncada Program seriously, their purpose being to deceive "everyone" in order to obtain power and thus declare "communism" in Cuba. The second asserts that Castro never intended to transform the revolution to socialism but was obliged to do so and to enter into his alliance with the Soviet Union. Ethical considerations aside, both these interpretations are implausible. Castro and a small group of revolutionary leaders did indeed have a Marxist understanding of history and a socialist *vocation*. However, to argue that this inevitably predetermined the course of the Cuban revolutionary process is to assume that history develops from the plotting of an elite operating in a vacuum. That a group of persons with similar ideologies constituting a party or a political movement should have come together in a systematic way to discuss what course to follow is nothing new; the question is whether a few men could have made history at their whim if reality had been averse to their vision. What the theorists propose to us in each of the above-mentioned hypotheses is that such a thing is credible. No political program that seeks broad consensus can situate itself beyond that consensus. This has been considered elementary by every politician from Lenin to Reagan. No man or group of men can generate historical change on the scale of that of Cuba on the basis of conspiracy on the margin of, and even against, the will of the majority of the nation.

The Moncada Program may have been inadequate to the socialist aspirations and ideals of Fidel Castro and other leaders, but it was the most advanced one possible for launching the struggle against tyranny and reviving the historic pursuit of sovereignty and independence. Whatever the result of the debate about the nature of the struggle against Batista (civil or armed), the definitive direction had to be made clear by reality. Batista blocked any possibility of an exclusively political-civil struggle, and this permitted radicalization in favor of armed struggle. The

United States, for its part, showed only a few weeks after the revolutionary triumph in 1959 that it would not tolerate the initiation of any such program as that described in *La historia me absolverá* (Castro, 1953). Upon the signing of the agrarian reform law (which was moderate even compared with that proposed in the 1980s for El Salvador), President Dwight Eisenhower authorized Operation Pluto, which was to have its denouement on the sands of the Bay of Pigs. As the Cuban leaders had predicted, the axiom of "limited sovereignty" for Latin American countries relative to Washington's interests prevailed once again with regard to the triumphant revolution. Under the circumstances, the apparently reformist and moderate Moncada Program became profoundly revolutionary, since it could remain viable only through the most radical choices.

The United States already had in 1959 a long list of military interventions and promotions of *coups d'état* in this hemisphere without any real relation to their struggle to "contain communism." One after another, presidents or popular leaders whose aspirations for change and social justice had never questioned their compatibility with a capitalist social and economic structure were overthrown or assassinated. From Sandino to Arbenz the United States had been consistent in its predilection for exercising a model of hegemony based on domination and intolerance. The Cuban case was to be no exception.

Given the direct confrontation between the United States and the Moncada Program, the alternatives for those who had fought Batista under that banner were either to give in to Washington and the national oligarchies and become yet another government in republican history or to cling to that banner, accepting the radicalization required to survive the North American challenge. In the exchange of blows the process moved forward—now with the acceptance and militant support of the broad masses—toward the socialist option. Under the new circumstances it had become evident that not even a moderate project could survive the intolerance of the United States and its allies in the local oligarchy, and only socialism could make the Moncada Program feasible. The apparent "change of direction" toward socialism was in fact a revolutionary continuity preconditioned by reality.

This somewhat prolonged historical discussion is necessary to clarify the discussion. It is the combination of North American intolerance of anything beyond limited sovereignty for Cuba in 1959, the socialist vocation of the Cuban leaders, and the people's will to fight in defense of the nation and its interests that explains the possibility of the radicalization of the process and the socialist option. To the extent that the Moncada Program was unrealizable without the socialist option, those who opposed the latter amounted to traitors to that program and more or less shamelessly aligned themselves with the United States. At the same time, no one requested the consent and support of the Soviet Union in undertaking the socialist option—although the later Soviet decision to offer support and cooperation was undoubtedly decisive in making that option viable. Given the national and international circumstances of 1959, only a socialist revolution could generate the internal and external alliances necessary to carry out the Moncada Program, consolidate Cuban independence and sovereignty, mobilize resources for social development, and establish the genuinely national and international stature of the republic.

From all of this, however, another reality is inferred: Socialism in Cuba—as everywhere but perhaps here especially dramatically—emerges not as a result of the long cultural, political, and productive preparatory process that Karl Marx predicted but as a classist option for defending a given form of social development in the context of a confrontation with a hostile power that is geographically close and hegemonic economically, financially, militarily, culturally, and politically—a power that, incidentally, happened to be and still is the greatest in history. It is in light of the *necessity* of the socialist option and the lack of "preparation," in the historical sense, for its undertaking that the partial results of three decades of revolutionary process in Cuba must be measured.

Socialism: Ideals and Realities

If we contrast Marx's vision of the advent of socialism with the way in which it finally came about, we note an appreciable gap between the theoretical conception and the reality in which it was objectified decades later. Socialism was not a natural outgrowth of the logic of the most developed capitalism but a necessary though premature and forced outgrowth of peripheral, backward, and deformed capitalism.

For Marx—who did not live to experience imperialism under advanced capitalism—the capitalist organization of society, having at first meant a revolutionary and extraordinary leap in the development of technology and production, would eventually become a hindrance to the latter and generate a historical stagnation that would produce tensions inevitably leading to social revolution. It would be the proletariat that would, because of its objective situation, be called upon to make the revolution, to abolish private property, and to initiate a new historical era with the elimination of classes. This vision conceived of such a revolution as the work not of a vanguard party but of the whole of the working class; it supposed not the isolated triumph of the revolution in one country or another but a "worldwide" revolution; it did not involve a long process of economic development competing with developed capitalist powers, since the latter were supposed to be the very places in which revolution would occur. Nor did it conceive of a prolonged phase of dictatorship in order to defend the revolutionary triumph from its internal and external enemies, since it assumed a "universal" triumph of the proletariat. By the end of the past century it had become evident that, although it might follow the general direction predicted by Marx, history was not to take that course.

Under the conditions of the imperialist era, the developed capitalist center was able to evade its problems of accumulation and along with them the social tensions often emerging from its own restructuring and the plundering of peripheral countries. It was in the latter that the revolutionary crisis was developed. The necessity of change was a given not because the capitalist system was running out of development possibilities but because the peripheral capitalism in which these possibilities were immersed impeded a capitalist development like that of nineteenth-century Europe or North America and because the imperialist policy toward peripheral countries precluded the minimal independence they required for reform. In these circumstances, it was clear that the barrier to economic development was not private ownership of the local means of production but a whole set of structures deformed by foreign hegemony. As various reform movements and leaders failed or were defeated in their efforts to increase their independence to effect a change within a capitalist framework, the option of breaking with the world capitalist system under a socialist conception became attractive to the most backward peoples. Nationalism and socialism fused, the latter being the only thing that could make the former viable.

However, the historical socialism that we have known since 1917 could not develop Marx's theoretical ideals fully and without trauma. Its emergence was forced, and the context was in no way propitious for its normal survival and growth. The hostile and threatening reality that socialism had to face definitively marked its praxis, causing dramatic adjustments to the theoretical project that affected the course of its development. The historical choice, however, was clear: It was either capitalist underdevelopment or that socialism, whatever its limitations, as a possibility not only for economic development but also for social and political development that might gradually open the way for socialist forms closer to Marx's theoretical project. The nascent real socialism was called on to realize a transition to Marxism's ideal socialism, from which one could then advance toward the communist vision that appeared on the misty horizon.

For the adversaries and enemies of that project the inevitable objective was either returning to the situation under capitalism or ensuring, by means of an aggressive policy, that the nascent socialism, in order to survive, would have to undertake a course of economic and political action that would warp its identity and cause it to lose itself in the maze of the transition, never to arrive at more fully socialist forms. The history of these seven decades of socialism in the world and of the last three of revolutionary praxis in Cuba are indelibly marked by that confrontational context, and it is in that context that one must examine the results.

The peoples that opted for socialist revolution as the only way of ensuring their independence and thus their development had consequently two main interconnected strategic objectives: to move from a poor agricultural civilization to a modern contemporary industrial one and to achieve that transformation under a socialist culture (social organization). Those that, under the pressure of the tasks of survival, consolidation of power, and accelerated industrialization, lost sight of the necessity of employing socialist forms of social organization ran the risk that instead of "constructing socialism" they would end up with developed capitalism in more or less socialist forms. If this wrong turn from the rocky path of the transition were taken, socialism historically understood would be an "accident" in the course of the development of world capitalism, even a form of development of an inferior level of capitalism.

Cuban Revolutionary Praxis: System and Models

An assessment of three decades of revolutionary power in Cuba must take into account the historical context just described and consider its efficacy in attaining the two strategic objectives that it imposed upon itself when it chose the socialist path. Consequently, there are three key areas to examine: the national and international conditions during the emergence and development of Cuban revolutionary power; *in that context,* the results in terms of consolidating the nation's independence, sovereignty, and international stature and in terms of economic and social development; and, once again *in that context,* the degree to which the praxis of the revolution has approximated the construction of a socialist society as close as possible to Marx's ideal.

It is pertinent to clarify from the start that my proposed methodology is not an excuse for an apologia. On both sides of the ideological barricades there are those who have learned to make the half-truth a way of life. In the debate over the Cuban Revolution there are those who, resorting to the undeniable expedient of ongoing U.S. aggression, glorify the work of those years, obscuring its intrinsic deficiencies. Nor has there been any lack of those who would ignore or minimize that factor in an often self-serving effort to denigrate the revolutionary undertaking. I take the historical context to mean not just the Cuba–United States dynamic but the sum total of the national and international factors that constitute the environment of Cuban revolutionary activity. I do not attempt to justify every Cuban decision on the basis of the description of that environment, but I do consider it a necessary point of reference for an understanding of the perceptions and reasoning—correct or erroneous—in terms of which Cuban praxis was shaped.

With these indispensable caveats we can proceed to look at some of the most general characteristics of the context in which the Cuban Revolution emerged and developed.

On the international level, the United States was at the apogee of its global hegemony in all its spheres (financial, industrial, military, and diplomatic). Latin America, in contrast, found itself linked with and economically, politically, and militarily subject to the interests of Washington, which employed (and continues to employ) a model of hegemony and leadership based on domination and control of Latin American events in terms of the principle of "limited sovereignty" for those countries. The "Arbenz syndrome" accompanied Latin American revolutionary thought in the examination of projects and options. The Third World in general had scarcely emerged from colonialism and was still trying, for instance, in the Bandung Conference of 1956, to define its identity and examine its development alternatives. The Soviet Union and the European socialist countries (recently reconstructed after World War II), along with China, were experiencing a notable technology gap relative to the West, an equally unfavorable military disequilibrium, and very limited finances. At the same time, the Soviet Union's nuclear arms capacity and its recently acquired ability to transport them via guided missiles marked the beginning of cumulative change in the international military balance. This new condition, together with its firmness in international crises such as those involving the Suez and Berlin, lent the Soviet Union substantial international influence in those years of the Cold War and precarious world equilibrium.

On the national level, Cuba was economically dependent on North American technology, financing, products, raw materials, and markets for its development. As an agricultural country, it had only isolated, small-scale industries for the internal market and imported the majority of its essential industrial and consumer goods. Its general infrastructure was inadequate and outmoded. Though an island nation, it had neither a fishing nor a merchant fleet. The performance of its long chain of governments oscillated between despotism and authoritarianism; politics was a corrupt and violent way of life in which anything was permissible as long as the interests of the national oligarchy were not affected and the limited sovereignty jealously guarded by every North American ambassador was not infringed upon (this latter was the real repository of all power). Cuban "foreign policy," like that of almost all Latin American countries of those years, was nonexistent, since in reality it was an exact reflection of that of the United States, whose diplomats sent precise instructions to Cuban representatives regarding its orientation. Of a population close to 6 million, 23.6 percent of those over ten years of age were illiterate and 1 million were semiliterate; six hundred thousand children had no schools and ten thousand teachers no work; there was only one industrial training center for midlevel technicians and only six centers for agricultural training with very limited capacity. Unemployment reached a level of one-third of the labor force (seven hundred thousand people) and was concentrated mostly in rural areas, and a level of development, as measured in terms of gross domestic product, in the medium range relative to the rest of Latin America concealed a social reality of critical inequality, the polarization of wealth having no relation whatsoever to the supposed per capita conditions that the figures suggested. Along with the numerous virtues accompanying the emergence and development of the Cuban nation, a set of social vices had come to permeate republican reality, including gambling, large-scale prostitution, loan-sharking, the systematic and institutionalized practice of patronage, and the corruption of political authorities at every level in order to obtain "favors" indispensable for subsistence (a bed in a hospital, money for a doctor or for the payment of household rent).

This—in bold strokes—was the reality that a political vanguard forged principally in a conspiratory military experience inherited. That vanguard was made up of men of diverse political and ideological tendencies and lacked the political organization capable of transforming the various organizations of selective and limited membership into a broad political party. The pillar of its defense was initially restricted to the victorious rebel army of workers and *campesinos*, largely semiliterate, with little discipline and primitive military technology. Its actions conditioned by that national and international reality, Cuba became the first country in this hemisphere to find a way—through its socialist option—successfully to challenge the axiom of its "limited sovereignty" and to transform itself in a radical way.

If the national "heritage" were not in itself sufficient reason to undertake a project of balanced and rapid development—not to mention the complexity arising from the high expectations of its socialist character—there were the United States and the counterrevolution that inevitably accompanies any genuine process of radical change, seeking to impede it at every turn and never abandoning the effort to return the Cuban revolutionary reality to its previous status. By way of a brief inventory, let us recall what it meant for revolutionary Cuba to have to reorient its market, replace its technology in virtually all areas, adapt its production to new goods, and run the country in the midst of a massive flight of its professionals, from physicians to engineers. No other Latin American country seeking reform while also having to face such economic reprisals could have survived intact. But, of course, that was not the only setting for the confrontation. The organizing, training, and equipping of counterrevolutionary terrorists was the first stage of an escalation in which the United States tested all manner of weapons: sabotage, assassination, irregular warfare, pirate incursions targeting production centers, mercenary invasion with U.S. naval and air cover, and nuclear threat.

Given this situation, the opportune help of the Soviet Union was decisive in the defense of Cuban revolutionary power, but it would have been insufficient if it had not been accompanied by the people's desire to triumph. If we were to measure the Cuban Revolution only by its capacity to survive—its creativity in finding ways of establishing its independence and sovereignty in the face of an uncommon adversary—words would fail us. Moreover, it was not just a matter of survival but one of developing the country *on the basis of social justice, within a socialist framework.*

If indeed the ultimate objective of the United States toward Cuba has always been to put an end to revolutionary power (including its socialist orientation), no less important in its policy has been ensuring the persistence of a set of circumstances that will impede its economic, social, and political development. Blockade and military threat have been constants of U.S. policy toward Cuba. In a word, if the revolution could not be defeated, that policy aimed to ensure that it could not develop the country, deliver the promised social benefits, or elaborate a political model of popular democracy and would have to function in a permanent state of economic and military emergency. If it proved impossible to crush the revolution by tactical means, it would be necessary to make it fail through strategic means. To this would be added, of course, a policy of isolation and distortion of the revolution's work by highlighting its dark side and obscuring its light.

The revolutionary Cubans have had to struggle for their ideals these thirty years not only because of the historical shortcomings mentioned above but also because of the challenge of survival both as a political power and as a socialist project. Those from the left who call after three decades for an ideal socialism that no one has been able to achieve under better circumstances and minimize or ignore the difficult realities are asking for a utopian paradise that does not exist. The truly meritorious thing about the Cuban Revolution is that it has never accepted the statement that "politics is the art of the possible" but has attempted "the impossible" a thousand times in order to be sure that, in the end, it would know what the limits were.

Cuba today can display social indicators that would be the envy of any other country in the Third World and, for some, even of developed countries. Even those who would denigrate the accomplishments of the revolution cannot deny that Cuba is one of the few countries in the world where no citizen of any age, sex, or color is without shelter, where no matter what the fluctuation of the level of consumption each person is guaranteed a minimum of subsistence and a stable income to pay for daily needs, where sickness is not a twin tragedy, both physical and economic, and where access to the highest levels of education and culture is determined not by level of income but by talent.

At the same time, the Cuban Revolution *democratized* the nation not simply by establishing mechanisms of popular democratic participation but by *democratizing the structure of power* that underlies every political system and determines what interests set the priorities for its functioning. While democracy in capitalist society is taken to mean the consensus of the citizens, expressed cyclically at the polls, in favor of alternative projects over whose elaboration they have little influence, in Cuba consensus is expressed not only at the polls but through active social participation that, were it not genuine, could not have supported revolutionary power for three decades. If the threatening proposals of the Santa Fe I Program and the history revolving around "going to the source" had to be smoothed over, it was because—imperialist propaganda aside—it was recognized that Cubans exercise their revolutionary socialist option with rifles at hand and that their differences over possible alternatives for the construction of the new society are accompanied by a solid consensus in favor of the new society that we are building.

The Cuban democratic system includes legal equality but goes beyond it, encompassing as well the economic and social rights of citizens without which the exercise of legal equality is basically enjoyed by only a minority of the people. What meaning can democracy have for the estimated 60 million marginalized people who survive from day to day in contemporary Brazilian society? How effective has representative democracy been in Latin America in affording the minimum conditions of decent existence for all of its citizens and not just a small group? How successful has democracy been as a political system under the conditions of capitalism, whether developed or underdeveloped, in preventing homelessness and guaranteeing its population jobs, health, and education?

Our democracy is an imperfect and developing political system influenced, furthermore, by the ongoing confrontation with the United States. Its deficiencies or limitations (some necessary, others unnecessary) have occasionally given rise to grave anomalies in the process as it unfolds and to a degree blocked the full use of the participatory potential offered by the socialist system. However, while we are tackling the problem of reinforcing the democratic character of our institutions, recognizing that we have not achieved perfection in our political system, we consider our participatory democracy to be supported by a structure of power that is equally democratic as and much more desirable and satisfactory than a "market democracy" in which the political-legal system is based on a polarized and asymmetrical structure of economic and financial power.

Democracy is a political *procedure* for attaining ends such as social justice. Without denying the deficiencies of a political system that is still evolving, we accept the challenge of comparing our democracy with any other in the attainment of those ends. The vast majority of our citizens are united behind the tasks of economic development and participate equally in the struggle to perfect the political system. That same immense majority defends that imperfect economic and political system in evolution against the alternative of a reorganization under capitalism.

In the international arena, the revolution has permitted the nation to assume a prestigious and influential place in the international community. Its foreign policy has been based from the start on ethical principles and practiced in a consistent and coherent way no matter what the crisis confronted. Cuba's prestige despite multiple diplomatic pressures to minimize it is evidenced in the number of high positions that it has been elected to hold in international forums. From the presidency of the influential movement of nonaligned nations to membership in the Security Council of the United Nations, Cuba has performed—with broad recognition—the most diverse and complex tasks in the diplomatic sphere.

No less significant are the results of its civil and military aid to other countries. The fact that a small country, the target of a policy producing the flight of half of its physicians in a few short months, should now be capable of having more doctors in the Third World than the World Health Organization clearly illustrates not only the Cuban cultural advance but the ethic that accompanies its foreign policy as well. Also significant has been the military assistance offered to Ethiopia and Angola in defending their territorial integrity from foreign threats. That Namibia was moved toward independence is due in large part to the participation of our young combatants, who together with the Angolans defeated the armed forces of Pretoria in the battle of Cuito Cuanavale.

This brief summary of thirty years of Cuban revolutionary praxis in a context plagued by dangers, pressures, and difficulties leaves an unquestionably favorable balance when analyzed in the light of its socialist option and in contrast with the experience of countries that pursued their development through peripheral capitalism. This is by no means to say that the Cuban trajectory is devoid of vulnerabilities and mistakes, that there have been no detours or profound adjustments in its ongoing adaptation and struggle for survival and development, or that immoralities have not stained a work whose historical stature rises above any excrescence. Overcoming such problems is not a matter of questioning the socialist system on the mistaken assumption that they are inherent in it but a matter of discussing and revising the model with a view to the rectification and improvement of Cuban society.

What is often presented—repeating the self-criticisms of Cuban revolutionaries themselves—as a crisis of socialism is really a set of critical symptoms of the exhaustion of one model of how it might function. That model was gradually transplanted from the European socialist experience during the 1970s and put an end to a period, lasting a little more than a decade, of intellectual and practical creative effort that characterized the revolution's search for a model of its own. In the field of economics it was characterized by an incipient reorientation toward the market mechanism and the economic thought that accompanies it. The cultural and political fields saw the rise of phenomena until then unknown to Cuban praxis, such as dogmatism, the bureaucratization of the work style of social and political organizations, the progressive tendency toward bureaucratic instead of democratic centralism, and the reintroduction of phenomena of social stratification, impunity, and the beginnings of bourgeois ideology in certain sectors and groups in middle- and high-level positions. If any "crisis" exists in Cuba, it is not one of consensus around the socialist option under the direction of the Party but the crisis of a model that increasingly threatens the socialist nature of our system and the authority of that Party.

When today it is said that the revolution seeks to isolate itself from the socialist model that is currently being abandoned in various European countries, the reality of the Cuban situation is being distorted. Cuba does indeed desire—and may have been a pioneer in saying so—to divorce itself from that model, unfortunately transplanted to a context foreign to it. What Cuba does not desire is to replace it with another imported socialist model that does not meet its needs, and much less does it wish to look to capitalism as a possible solution to the problems it faces. Cuba is in *motion*, but it wants to move in a *socialist and Cuban* direction this time around.

The problems we face today are also largely a result of the success— not of the failure—of these three revolutionary decades. Our problem today is not to teach people to read and write but to make efficient use of each person's talents, not how to employ a third of the labor force but how to increase productivity, not importing new industries but making the most advantageous use of the capacity we have, not creating organs of popular power and participation but freeing the existing ones from bureaucratic obstacles to their full use, not promoting a sense of unity and discipline about a revolutionary project but regulating the political space necessary for its discussion and its ongoing examination and correction.

The inevitable traumas that were generated by the discovery of drug trafficking among a small group of the Cuban military and corruption in the upper ranks of the Ministry of the Interior *do not put in doubt the course of rectification undertaken by the revolution but underline the necessity of accelerating and deepening it.* The milieu and conceptions that led to these phenomena were engendered before and not after the start of the rectification of the revolutionary course, and their detection corroborates the dangers for Cuban socialism under its former orientation.

Conclusions

The outcome of Cuban praxis in the last thirty years confirms the legitimacy of the socialist option as a sine qua non for the consolidation of independence and for the initial steps toward social development. In contrast with the positive and radical transformation of the Cuban scene, attempts at development from the capitalist periphery in this hemisphere in the end have achieved fluctuating economic growth that does not extend to social development for the whole of the citizenry or guarantee its basic human needs. It is in this respect and not as a model to emulate in other historic junctures that the Cuban case constitutes a historic paradigm for Latin American efforts to achieve full independence and sovereignty and to generate integrated and stable development.

The Cuban Revolution, both in its efforts at social and economic development and in its attempt to construct a socialist society, has suffered and continues to suffer from inadequacies and limitations whose origin lies, on the one hand, in the context of the historical underdevelopment and confrontation with the United States from which it emerged and, on the other, in conceptual and practical errors committed throughout these three decades. The shortcomings, faults, and more or less serious errors associated with Cuban revolutionary praxis can generate criticism and even rejection without calling into question either the legitimacy of the totality of the work of these three decades or the historic dimension of the revolutionary process that is still evolving and developing.

The Cuban Revolution is currently involved in overcoming a model of operation that it imported from a European context in the past decade. The pernicious effects of its inheritance will be felt for some time to come by Cuban society, which is undertaking its rectification and reshaping its functional scheme from a perspective that is both socialist and Cuban.

References

Castro, Fidel. 1953. *La historia me absolverá.* Havana.

3

Political Culture and Popular Participation

Rafael Hernández and Haroldo Dilla

Translated by Jennifer Dugan Abbassi and Jean Díaz

Political culture is shared in a different way from ideology, being less consciously assimilated and therefore broader. In addition to systematizing a predominant ideology, the revolution has transformed Cuban culture and developed national values that, for lack of a better term, might be called a new civility.[1]

Most Cubans have experienced neither capitalism nor the hardest years of the revolution; scarcely 40 percent of the population over sixteen can recall that first stage. Their culture, like their ideology, is a result of new patterns of social relations brought about by the revolutionary process. As a consequence, state protection of individual and community rights, access to social life and work, and the opportunity for individual participation—the elements of this new civility that are the basis of social life—are part of the fabric of political culture. They are social values rather than ideological principles, although ideology can and does reinforce them.

This chapter examines the basis of a participatory political culture and discusses the extent to which new values lead to participation and by whom. A central focus will be the degree to which these participatory options represent real alternatives for expression and action.

Historical Roots of Cuban Political Culture

The first literary text that reflects Cuban culture, a seventeenth-century epic poem entitled *The Mirror of Patience* by Silvestre de Balboa, exemplifies two key aspects of Cuban political culture.[2] On the one hand, it reflects the great national diversity that has existed ever since the island's origin as a crossroads, including the early and active African component of national identity. On the other, it documents rebellion against both internal and external repression, underlining rejection of colonial domination and a united front against external enemies as radical features of cultural expression. These two elements constitute a worldview characteristic of Cuban culture from its inception.

Together with Puerto Rico, Cuba is one of the last of the Spanish possessions to have achieved independence from the metropolis. The War of Independence in Cuba occurred late in comparison with those in the rest of Latin America, and therefore it developed under a leadership and a political program, embodied by the revolutionary project of José Martí, that were more radical and advanced. The independence struggle ended under the direction of an organized political party whose platform articulated the struggle not only against Spain but also against the United States—and in fact it faced North American intervention in its final phase. In addition, foreigners—from Latin America, Europe, and the United States—participated in this struggle, and the top leadership positions were held by men who were descendants of slaves. The leader of the liberation army, General Máximo Gómez, was born in Santo Domingo. The second in command, General Antonio Maceo, son of a Venezuelan, was a mulatto. Thus a sense of progress, modern precepts, racial integration, multinational participation, capacity for prolonged struggle, national liberation, and confrontation with the young North American empire became part of national political culture in the very achievement of independence.

Whereas it is generally agreed that Cuba's political struggles in the first half of the twentieth century were motivated primarily by its position relative to the United States, the progressive historical effects of this position have received much less attention. Before the War of Independence, and especially from the end of the eighteenth century on, Cuba experienced substantial economic development, urbanization, and international visibility. Long before its liberation from Spain, its principal trading partner was the United States. The intense postwar influx of capital produced accelerated economic growth, modernization of the education and health systems, and technological advances in the mass media. Cuba produced its first movie in 1906. It was the second country in the hemisphere to have a television station, and its radio production was renowned throughout Latin America. A dynamic national economic life—alongside unemployment, monocrop production, the latifundio system, and the impoverishment of a considerable proportion of the population—reflected levels of profitability and efficiency more typical of advanced than of dependent capitalism. These patterns conditioned Cuba's incorporation into the world economy. Ironically, Cuban capitalism also contributed to the definition and formation of a more homogeneous national culture.

The evolution of Cuban political culture was further shaped by the relative dynamism of its popular movements. While the dominant political parties represented by the Cuban oligarchy were characterized by corruption, despotism, and illegitimacy, there were also popular political organizations and a tradition of labor struggles that achieved a high level of mobilization and generally high standards of political participation, especially in comparison with those in other countries in the region. And although the political game allowed for every kind of fraud, the last constitution, adopted in 1940, was one of the most advanced in the world to the extent that it was influenced by the popular movement of the 1930s.

Finally, Latin American political life has had active expression in Cuba. Throughout the twentieth century the island has been a refuge for the region's political exiles, and Cuban political movements have reflected the political struggles in Latin America and elsewhere. Men who fought side by side with Augusto César Sandino in Nicaragua died for the social revolution in Cuba during the 1930s. In relation to its population, Cuba's contribution to the international brigades in the war in Spain was the hemisphere's largest (the Abraham Lincoln Brigade from the United States being the most numerous in absolute terms). There were organized movements in Cuba to overthrow the dictator Rafael Trujillo of the Dominican Republic, to increase the forces of President Jacobo Arbenz in Guatemala, and in solidarity with the Colombia of Jorge Eliécer Gaitán. This current of political support extended and strengthened the supranational values of Cuban identity.

Mobilization and Socialization as Ingredients of Political Culture

Social relations in revolutionary Cuba are highly politicized. The penetration of the political into family life that was to some extent characteristic of traditional society intensified after the revolutionary triumph. Especially during the first half of the 1960s, politics was a cause of family polarization. Phenomena such as migration to the United States acquired an intense political connotation, independent of personal motivation.

To a large extent the rhythm of politicization reflects the use of the mass media as a means of political orientation and ideological education. Fidel Castro used television to discuss major national problems, orient the masses, explain the political situation, and even make public decisions.[3] This massive political education contributed to a rapid change in the culture of the population. The classic example is the dramatic spread, within barely two years of the triumph of the revolution, of popular knowledge about socialism and communism. The social program of the revolution and intensive political education altered the anticommunist sentiments of broad sectors of the population and allowed Castro to declare the revolution socialist in April 1961 and to identify himself as a Marxist-Leninist in December of the same year.

In the long run, the social program of the revolution, with its new system of values, brought with it the consolidation of certain notions that individuals acquire as part of their understanding of the new reality. This is reflected in such basic spheres as work. Most Cubans take it for granted that, whatever the country's economic situation, all citizens will be guaranteed jobs. Consequently, notions of a fixed income, social security, and the satisfaction of basic necessities have become part of the expectations of daily life. The transformation of work from a relation of exploitation to a more positive collectivist relation is a logical consequence of revolutionary change. Massive mobilizations for volunteer work are expressions of new attitudes toward the appropriation of the product of labor. Participation in productive tasks—especially in agriculture and construction—reflects a new concept of labor and social property. At the same time, phenomena such as lack of discipline and low productivity reveal negative attitudes toward work whose origins have been neglected in discussion on the sociological level. The question remains to what extent the availability of employment and the exclusion of forms of compulsion usually associated with a pattern of capitalist exploitation, together with errors in the conception and implementation of certain economic policies, have limited the development of a new work culture.

From the ideological point of view, the most conspicuous component of the new political culture is *equality*. This is not solely a theoretical position but also corresponds to the policies of the new regime—the extension of social services to the whole population either free of charge or at subsidized rates, equal access to basic consumer goods, the democratization of centers of work and study, and the elimination of all forms of institutional discrimination on the basis of race or sex.[4] Although "egalitarianism" is one of the tendencies of the 1960s that has since been judged idealistic, the criteria of social justice, democracy, and equity continue to dominate political culture. These values are fundamental to political consensus. At the same time, it is widely recognized that inequalities persist as a result of occupational, regional, or urban-rural differences or because they have been "dragged along from the past."[5] A true measure of these differences would, however, require consideration of a complex of economic and social aspects that affect the standard of living but are not expressed in a unidimensional indicator such as wages.[6]

Two other important and interconnected ideological components are *national defense* and *internationalism*. Revolution intensifies feelings of patriotism; additionally, North American policy toward Cuba has greatly contributed to the identification of national defense as a priority. Since 1959 this has come to symbolize the revolutionary cause itself and is one of the major motivations for mass mobilization. This means that the activities of national defense are part of everyday life. In general, people do not live in a constant state of alarm and mobilization, as in the 1960s, expecting a new crisis with the United States. There have, however, been periods, such as the early 1980s, of aggravated tensions and a corresponding increase in military mobilization.

Internationalist missions such as those to Angola and Ethiopia also intensify military activity. As has already been pointed out, the idea of combat in another country for a just cause—in particular, defense against foreign aggression—is an active element of Cuban political culture. The brevity of the armed struggle against the Batista regime and its heroic connotation left succeeding generations with a certain yearning for similar epic tasks; after the beginning of the 1960s these tasks became less frequent. The internationalist missions in Africa, considered as collective experiences, realized these values. In particular, the Latin American connection and the African heritage, as well as relations with the liberation movements that had come to power on that continent, were fundamental ideological issues in the 1960s and 1970s. While the wars in Africa have contributed to Cuba's massive military preparedness, the internationalist experience in Africa cannot be appreciated simply as a military feat. It has also had a fundamental cultural impact on Cuban life. More than three hundred thousand Cubans—including both service people and civilian delegations of doctors, builders, technicians, and teachers—have gone to Angola, thereby exposing hundreds of thousands of Cubans to the critical realities of the Third World. The levels of health care, nutrition, and education and the problems of economic development, natural limitations, national unity, social structure, and regional isolation that characterize the majority of African countries are alien to the Cuban context. Hardly any other country in the hemisphere has such broad, prolonged, and direct knowledge of the tragic reality of the Third World as Cuba. The same could be said of knowledge gained not through books but directly from the Soviet Union and other countries of Eastern Europe, where thousands of Cubans have studied or worked.

The literacy campaign launched in 1961 was aimed not only at teaching Cubans to read and write but also at providing essential political knowledge about national and international reality. The education process influences and reinforces the political agenda around which citizens are mobilized. Education becomes not only a goal of social policy but a representation of individual behavior. The slogan "He who does not study lags behind" points to the personalization of certain cultural values of the new civility.

Although access to foreign newspapers and magazines in Cuba is severely limited—and not only for economic reasons—there is a relative diversity of other media. For example, according to 1986 data, the variety of films shown in movie theatres alone included twenty films from North America, twenty-eight from the Soviet Union, and one hundred from Europe, in addition to twelve from Latin America and a few from Africa. This is in stark contrast to the majority of Latin American movie markets, which are dominated by the U.S. film industry. Even if restriction of the flow of information were a goal, it would be very difficult to achieve in a country like Cuba, whose strategic position at the entrance to the Gulf of Mexico and the Panama Canal, close to the United States, and between the two Americas exposes it to the radio signals of the entire hemisphere. Despite the virtual commercial blockade, young Cubans continue to be up on the Top 40 and the dance styles in vogue in the United States.

In contrast with other socialist countries, Cuba has had no official art. A look at the literature, plastic arts, and music created over the last thirty years reflects the assimilation of contemporary currents of talent and the space granted to experimental and avant-garde art. Socialist realism is simply one of many schools of art, not an official "state art." Deficiencies in the area of culture have had much more to do with administrative mechanisms and confusion than with any narrow political philosophy. In addition to greater participation in cultural activities for the ordinary citizen, the political culture incorporates diversity and what is new and worthy in artistic values and creation.

One final aspect of the new civility is social control and responsibility in the face of violations of the public order. In contrast to the indifference that prevailed in the prerevolutionary period, citizen vigilance over crime has emerged, in the framework of some revolutionary organizations, as an expression of a more responsible and participatory concept of life in a collectivity. To a large extent, this phenomenon is an expression of a cultural pattern more sensitive to the social order. Other aspects of it are spontaneous forms of communal organization at the neighborhood level that have no equivalents anywhere in Latin America.

In summary, political culture is realized in many loci. Workplaces, schools, neighborhoods, and political and mass organizations all play a role in the process of socialization. Individual citizens feel involved in all of these social arenas, which offer them opportunities for, and demand from them, a high level of dedication and commitment. We thus see the reinforcement of the political as part of a continuing cycle.

A Participatory Political System

The opening up of participation in Cuba has been conditioned by conjunctural and structural factors inherent in its socialist transition. Participation has been decisive not only because of the importance of popular support for economic and social transformation and the defense of national sovereignty but also because of the key role it plays in the transmission of new values, norms, and regulatory procedures of citizen action. At the same time, the possibility of this participation has been maintained by the constant renewal of the popular consensus that has helped the revolutionary political leadership to confront the dangers of formalism.

Entering its fourth decade, the revolution exhibits very high levels of popular involvement in its participatory mechanisms. For example, in 1986 the Comités de Defensa de la Revolución, involved in various tasks in the areas of health care, education, volunteer work, defense, citizen security, and other social activities, had 6.5 million members, representing 84 percent of the Cuban population over fourteen years of age. The Federación de Mujeres Cubanas, with its orientation toward the promotion and representation of the interests of women, attracted 3.1 million, 80 percent of the adult female population. The unions, united in the Central de Trabajadores de Cuba, had a membership of about 3 million workers, a little more than 99 percent of the national total. Millions of others were participating in various social organizations (for farm workers, students, and others) and in what can be considered a test case for any democratic system, the popular militias (*militias de tropas territoriales*).

The creation of Poder Popular and in particular its local branches in 1976 opened the way for citizen participation in the selection of representatives in local government and the systematic control of their representational behavior. In the election of 1986, a total of 6.7 million people (almost 98 percent of the eligible population) cast their ballots, while in October 1988 5.2 million, or about 77 percent of the population over sixteen, took part in accountability assemblies, the public meetings held biannually to assess the performance of the local authorities in satisfying the needs of the population.

Finally, the Partido Comunista de Cuba and the Unión de Jóvenes Comunistas (Union of Communist Youth, UJC) had a membership in 1986 of more than 1.1 million, or about 16 percent of the politically active population.

These numbers may not tell us very much about the quality of this participation, understood as the capacity of the citizen to discuss the making of public policy, to criticize that policy, and to be active in its implementation. From this we derive two analyses, more to identify the problems associated with the subject than to offer definitive conclusions.

The magnitude and sociopolitical impact of the participatory process in Cuba are evident, and so is the fact that it is much more comprehensive than elsewhere on the continent—but such comparisons can be sterile. In the first place, it is appropriate to recover for debate a premise that is almost self-evident: As in all contemporary societies, political participation in Cuba has its limitations. The nature of these limitations (or at least of their effects) can be found in the principal political documents and in the national press: weaknesses in the subsystem of information, bureaucratism, the persistence of a certain marginalization of some social groups, excessive administrative centralization, underutilization of participatory mechanisms as a consequence of the traumatic rejection of old styles of "politicking," and so on. To what extent these limitations are "objective" or "subjective" is not always easy to say. History has demonstrated that a "subjective" obstacle is usually more difficult to remove by force of political will than one classified as "objective." More interesting is that many of these limitations, even when they can be publicly explained as "distortions" and in fact are such with respect to the original purposes of any participatory structure, have to do with contradictions inherent in the socialist transformation and the concrete reality of the construction of a political system that, while inspired by the best of theories, faces the difficult test of daily life.

The construction of democracy in Cuba is not an exercise in constitutional engineering supported by a centuries-old institutional tradition but an all-encompassing project of social justice, development, national independence, and participatory opening marked by the positive and negative elements of the political culture and arising from one of the so-called weak links of capitalist domination. In this context, it is scarcely necessary to mention the variable of external aggression, which in the Cuban case has meant confronting in all kinds of ways the hostility of the North American superpower. To what extent this latter is involved in many of the limitations mentioned remains to be examined, but, historically, war, armed subversion and propaganda, economic aggression, and so on, have not gone hand in hand with democratic excellence. In the midst of such adversity, the Cuban Revolution has gradually been able to expand opportunities for participation and to incorporate into its program what is officially called "the continuing improvement of socialist democracy." It will be impossible to detail all of the many factors that have contributed to this result, but all of them could be described in terms of two key dimensions: the individual's capacity to participate and the possibility of his doing so.

The first dimension has its immediate referent in what has been called a process of "liberation from subjectivity" implicit in socioeconomic and political transformation that involves the destruction or erosion of a series of relationships of oppressive power—within the community, in management, in the family, in education, between races—that permeated prerevolutionary society.

At the same time, it is interesting to examine the character and the breadth of the revolutionary political call for participation. Broadly speaking, "politics" is any public decision-making activity with reference to the management of collective entities. In a more restricted sense, it is the struggle between classes and social sectors over power, particularly state power. Usually it is the latter definition that is used in official discourse and in the Cuban social sciences, and this is why numerous organizations and citizens' groups are called "social" when in fact they are political. This is no accident. A good part of revolutionary history has been characterized by politico-ideological confrontation, and from this has arisen the assumption on the part of both apologists and detractors that citizen participation means political-ideological identification with the system. In fact, it would not be very realistic to deny the relevance of the politico-ideological identification of the citizenry with the values of the system as a catalyst to participation, but neither would it be realistic to attempt to reduce participation to full understanding of those values. In fact, the political call for participation has been sufficiently broad and autochthonous in its objectives and values—social justice, increase in the standard of living, development, national sovereignty—and in its organizational aspects to involve people and sectors whose norms and aspirations do not coincide exactly with the ideological ends of the system.

One test of Cuban democracy is undoubtedly popular participation in the militias, which defend a national independence that was realized under socialism but is at the same time an element of local political culture no matter what the prevailing ideology. At the same time, the notion of a volunteer rather than a professional army is not alien to the Cuban historical tradition, the wars of liberation from 1868 to 1959 having been conducted by troops of this kind. Similarly, the participation of neighbors in tasks of social import—a hospital, a child care center, or a housing project—is difficult to reduce to any ideological characteristic of the citizen, being in fact motivated by other variables ranging from a sense of belonging to a community to a general sensitivity to collective needs.

In summary, while political ideology is reflected in participation, the revolution as a process affects the political culture, which is manifested in various forms of social action.

Citizens, Mechanisms, and Areas of Participation

Everyone realizes his or her daily life in various settings—the center of work or study, the neighborhood, and so on—and in each of these there are specialized mechanisms of participation ranging from those that are selective and precisely defined ideologically, such as a cell of the Party or the Unión de Jóvenes Comunistas, to others in which ideology is of no great importance, such as the neighborhood council. The intensity of daily life in Cuba confronts citizens with more than one area and numerous formal and informal mechanisms of participation, with the result that their political involvement acquires a multifaceted character and is not always balanced with regard to the quality of participation in each area. For example, a woman who is active in her workplace as a union member may at the same time participate in the Comité de Defensa, the Federación de Mujeres, the neighborhood council, the council of her children's school, etc. In addition she may participate in activities related to Poder Popular and the militia and in informal activities of support and direct democracy. Even assuming that in each of these mechanisms she performs line functions and that in some she does so only formally, in accordance with her personal motivations, this list suggests a very active participant indeed. Moreover, this is a hypothetical person who is neither involved in the Party or the Unión de Jóvenes Comunistas nor studying (as is one-third of the adult population). The idea that every citizen can be an active participant in every organization and setting is attractive but probably not very realistic.

This presents a very complex problem that is as yet unresolved by contemporary Cuban sociology: the diverse relations that a citizen may maintain with the various areas and participatory mechanisms in which daily life unfolds. What makes an individual more active in one area than in another? We could come up with a series of hypothetical answers, certainly no one sufficient in and of itself. One thing that merits some study, then, is the participatory quality of each area and mechanism, beginning with that which can generate self-recognition as an active and not simply a formal participant in decisions.

As a means of exploring this, we may compare two basic participatory areas of present-day Cuban society, the workplace and the residential community, and specifically the two organizations within these that channel participation, the labor unions and Poder Popular.

In every Cuban workplace, participation is linked in some way to the existing union organization, the aim being the gradual development of forms of administrative partnership and an increase in production and productivity. Beginning with the thirteenth congress of the CTC in 1973, a set of mechanisms has been refined that involves the internal democratization of the unions by means of the periodic election of members to leadership positions, oversight of their work by the membership, and the right of the membership to recall them. The effect has been to open up an area of free discussion of problems internal to the organization in each unit through periodic assemblies and the right to criticize.

Although the content of property relations in this country and the nature of politics (and political style) in fact limit the possibility of major conflicts between labor and management, this does not mean that their relations are entirely harmonious. In fact a series of mechanisms has been designed to defend the everyday interests of workers, among them the workers' councils (elected by and made up of workers and called upon to resolve labor disputes) and practices such as the allocation by the workers' assembly of scarce consumer goods (household appliances, motor vehicles) in accordance with the merits (in terms of labor) of applicants. Finally, within a system of highly centralized planning, mechanisms of partnership have been created to enable workers and their representatives to take an active role in decision making and implementation in relation to the plan. Under this heading fall the production and service assemblies held periodically in each unit, the participation of union leaders in management councils, and the participation of workers in the design and/or application of technological innovations.

This inventory is of course incomplete, but it will suffice to reveal a very intense and complex participatory framework in the enterprise and a power in Cuban unions that is difficult to find in other parts of the continent. As might have been expected, however, in real life not all of these mechanisms appear to have been equally successful in practice, and this has turned the Cuban enterprise into an area of insufficient participation with respect not only to what might be desirable but also to what was planned.

The most relevant shortcomings probably lie in the functioning of the above-mentioned mechanisms aimed at the development of forms of administrative partnership. This is no accident: What is at issue is precisely the opening up of participation in a very sensitive aspect of the economy and its planning whose variables cannot always be controlled by the force of political will. At the same time, not all of the causes of the partial frustration of this project can be relegated to the inaccessible sphere of the necessary and the objective.

The employment of production and service assemblies to control the progress of the economic management plan goes back to the beginnings of the revolution. Given the high degree of centralization in economic decision making, their impact has been limited to the creation of an economic consciousness in the producers-owners of the means of production. After 1976, with the implementation of the Sistema de Dirección y Planificación de la Economía (System of Direction and Planning of the Economy, SDPE)—which involved large doses of managerial autonomy and decision making—these assemblies were called upon to become an axis of the more ambitious practice of partnership hailed by the fourteenth congress of the CTC in 1978. Whereas in that year production and service assemblies were held in only 65 percent of workplaces, by 1985 the figure was 97 percent. Subsequent appraisals by the fifteenth (1984) and the sixteenth (1990) congresses have indicated, however, that this is more a matter of quantitative than one of qualitative advance.

Just as the SDPE's program of decentralization was realized only in part, and in more than one case with unwanted results, the goal of democratizing the economic plan was eroded by bureaucratic-centralist tendencies, and the mechanisms intended to effect it fell victim to the evils of formalism. Discussion of the plan with the workers was regularly based on general figures lacking any practical concreteness and detached from the daily activity of the workers; moreover, they did not include vital economic measures and reached the rank and file only belatedly. The opinions and suggestions of the workers had no great impact on the final designs, and the fact that reasons for rejecting a proposal tended not to be offered generated, according to the participants in the fifteenth congress, "a justifiable irritation on the part of the workers." The union newspaper was much more conclusive: "The planning of the economy in Cuba has been characterized by a tendency toward bureaucratization and formality."

Although reliable empirical evidence is insufficient, from the public evaluation carried out so far it is possible to conclude that the results may be more satisfactory in enterprises that are larger and probably have a more deeply rooted labor tradition than in smaller ones and in administrative and service units. In any case, the process of change that is currently taking place in the country—known as rectification—shows signs of a political will directed more toward the creation of organizational conditions and procedures external to the unions (decentralization of management, creation of new areas of participation in the control of production, and so on) as well as within them (debureaucratization, development of a more active role, emergence of new leadership) that should lead to a qualitative and quantitative expansion of the existing areas of participation.

The second participatory area, the community, comprises a complex framework of diverse organizations, some with very specific political goals, others more concerned with social advancement, some with a mass base and others confined to specific social sectors. Among these, some (e.g., the CDRs, the FMC) are national in scope, but along with these there is a series of voluntary associations including school councils, neighborhood councils, clubs for young people and for the elderly, professional associations, associations of handicapped persons, cultural councils, and recreational groups. The way in which these associations are incorporated into politics and related to each other has not yet been examined. Instead of providing an inventory of this framework, therefore, we will examine in some detail the institutions that may be considered the participatory axis of the majority of Cuban communities: the local organs of Poder Popular, specifically those on the municipal level.

Although not free of difficulties, the participatory process generated around Poder Popular seems today to show a balance of significant success, despite the contrast with its ambitious design, in confronting the inevitably complex "diffuse rights" of citizens. Some of the various reasons for this are historical—for example, the precedent of Cuban municipal life and, after the revolution, of the CDRs and the brief experiment with Poder Local (Local Power)—but we do not believe that they can be reduced to these. By way of a hypothesis we might point to others (of course open to discussion) that have to do with the design of the project itself.

In the first place, the very simplicity of the governmental structures and participatory mechanisms and the sense of nativeness about them have facilitated learning and internalization of them on the part of citizens. In the second place, and closely related, in this combination of practices of direct democracy with technical representative ones it is the former that are preeminent by virtue of a certain attachment to the principles of the imperative mandate, which at the same time assumes very dynamic flows of information (ascending and descending) and considerable demystification of the techno-bureaucracy. Last, the town council was endowed with the powers necessary to transform demands into public policies and to generate sufficient output to reproduce its own legitimacy.

This may be the explanation for the high indices of participation that Poder Popular displays at the grass-roots level within only a little more than a decade of its introduction. In addition to electoral behavior, the popular response to the various calls for participation of Poder Popular is highly relevant. The cycle of accountability assemblies in 1980 (ending in October) included a total of 21,186 neighborhood assemblies, attended by 5.2 million people, a little more than 70 percent of the population over sixteen years of age. From these assemblies arose more than one hundred thousand ideas, 64 percent of which had to do with eight items in the areas of public services, retail trade, production of basic consumer goods, transportation, public health, and education. At the height of this cycle of neighborhood meetings there had accumulated (from prior meetings or from individual contacts of voters with their city representatives) a total of 458,000 demands, of which 75 percent were met either with assignments of material resources or with organizational measures, while explanations were offered to the affected citizens with regard to the issues that remained unresolved. This is not, however, to say that the responses of the administrative agencies have always been sufficient to meet the demands of the population.

Of course, if the appraisal of Poder Popular is limited to these figures it will be reduced to a benefactor status that certainly could not have stood the test of time in a society in which demands increase and grow more complicated as the basic needs are satisfied. It is no exaggeration to say that its effectiveness has lain in its having fostered active participation by the population in very dissimilar tasks. On the one hand, Poder Popular directly articulates with the community's institutional framework and from this generates, without detriment to the specific functions of each institution, a set of actions of support, criticism, and mobilization. Logically, the possibility of doing this with more or less success depends on various factors, among them the capacity of neighborhood leaders to achieve flexible and consensual calls for participation, but it is necessary to note that probably in this instance the potential is greater than the actuality. On the other hand, Poder Popular offers the ordinary citizen the possibility of carrying out tasks and assuming functions of high quality. In fact, more than thirteen thousand people serve as delegates to municipal assemblies, and the functions of these assemblies involve many ordinary people in tasks such as inspections and the elaboration of proposals concerning matters vital to community life. It is calculated that in October 1987 some nineteen hundred commissions assigned to these assemblies produced some four thousand reports and official opinions involving the work of more than twenty thousand people.

Obviously this optimistic perspective about community participation cannot be uniformly applied across the national spectrum. The results of this project have been more marked in the smaller communities than in the large cities. Here there seems to be a convergence of causal factors such as a policy of regional development that tends to privilege the interior at the expense of the capital and certain peculiarities of the design of Poder Popular that facilitate more efficient performance by the local authorities of small and medium-sized communities. Probably, however, other factors of long standing intervene as well, among them the existence of a more solid and therefore more deeply rooted community tradition in the provinces, especially in the more densely populated central municipalities. The very terms by which the local organs are designated is an indication of this difference: The people of Havana call the local organ Poder Popular, while the people of the interior call it "the government."

Final Considerations

The political culture of Cubans today reproduces and amplifies a historical tradition at the same time as it is nourished by the fundamental changes the revolution has wrought. The question remains to what extent this culture, bearer of active elements that affect participation, is finding an opportunity for full realization in the functioning of the political system—in other words, to what extent, given a (political) cultural predisposition to participation, organic, institutional, systematic national participation or, better, mobilized, direct local participation has been achieved.

Another cardinal problem is, obviously, the link between participation and real power. To participate is not simply to have access to multiple areas of discussion but to contribute to decision making in these areas. Participation in discussion and execution is relatively high; in political decisions and their control it is considerably less. Under ideal conditions, direct democracy would solve the problem. In the actual circumstances of a country such as Cuba, centralization of a number of important aspects of policy making seems to be a necessity. The problem is rooted in the effective functioning of the distinct levels of participation and decision making and especially in the correlation between "the government" and the Government.

The process of rectification that has been developing since 1986 has helped to call attention to the critical examination of the deficiencies of such basic organs as those of Poder Popular and the National Assembly. It has been pointed out that the former suffers from formalism and other inadequacies and that the latter, as the largest representation of popular power, should be more effective and active in its debates and in its capacity to control the organs of the state with the aim of solving the country's main problems. The fourth Party congress has called for greater popular control over governmental activities (PCC, 1990:16).

The very evolution of citizens' political culture under the impact of the revolution has essentially modified the conditions for the exercise of participatory democracy and popular power in Cuba. The Cuban citizenry, independently of its ideological diversity, shares a complex political culture born of the country's singular historical experience and developed and refined over three decades and has achieved a superior capacity for political discernment. These values, reinforced or constructed by the revolutionary process, are the fundamental substrate of potential change.

Notes

1. This term is not to be taken as equivalent to "civic culture," based on descriptive categories such as civic virtue, pluralist democracy, rational bureaucracy, and stability (see Almond and Verba, 1963:4–11).

2. See Vitier (1982). This poem relates the singular history of a group of creoles of various national origins—Spaniards, Italians, Portuguese, Jews, Dutch—

in the area of the eastern port of Manzanillo who defied the colonialist laws on commercial monopoly. The creole smugglers confronted a band of pirates that had kidnapped the bishop Juan de las Cabezas Altamirano. The hero of the poem is the black slave Salvador Golomón, who succeeds in freeing the bishop and killing the pirates' captain, the Frenchman Gilberto Girón.

3. In the United States John F. Kennedy, in 1960, was the first president to make effective political use of television (see Goodwin, 1988).

4. In Cuba medical attention and hospital care, education at all levels, athletic clubs and events, and funerals, among other services, are free, and prices are low for books, cultural events and entertainment, basic foodstuffs, housing (as a proportion of income), and public transport.

5. The denunciation of veiled forms of discrimination affecting blacks, women, and youth and the criticism of nepotism and corruption by certain leaders clearly reflect assaults on the value of equality (see PCC, 1986).

6. The prevailing wage policy in Cuba allows wages for different occupations to differ—for example, a construction worker may earn more than a professor, not to mention a skilled worker such as a carpenter or an electrician. A master craftsman or a professional (with the possible exception of a doctor) does not necessarily live better than a laborer. The income of a peasant landowner and his family who live in a remote area and generally lack many of the services available in the city is certainly higher than that of any state employee, and the children of such a peasant family may well become doctors or artists. On the other hand, a youth born in a predominantly black neighborhood in a city such as Havana, with access to all the social services just mentioned (especially education), is more likely to fall into antisocial behavior (delinquency) than the son of an agricultural worker living in a rural community. In summary, the assessment of differences in the quality of life requires broader elaboration and interpretation.

References

Almond, G., and S. Verba. 1963. *The Civic Culture.* Princeton: Princeton University Press.

Goodwin, Richard. 1988. *Remembering America.* Boston: Little, Brown.

PCC (Partido Comunista de Cuba). 1986. *Documentos del Tercer Congreso.* Havana.

———. 1990. *Llamamiento al IV Congreso.* Havana: Política.

Vitier, Cintio. 1982. *Lo cubano en la poesía.* Havana: Letras Cubanas.

4

Political Leadership in Cuba

Georgina Suárez Hernández

Translated by Aníbal Yáñez

The triumph of the Cuban Revolution marked the beginning of a new type of leadership linked to a course unprecedented in Cuba—the participation of the broadest social sectors in political life. This chapter begins its examination of this proposition with a review of the institutional foundation established by the revolution, including the new national state and the political system and the revolutionary measures that gave the people access to the economy, provided for social needs, and offered the opportunity for participation through mass organizations. It goes on to consider institutionalized participation in the state administration through the system known as Poder Popular. Finally, it offers an assessment of the single party, the harmful effects of economistic policies, and the positive changes effected by the rectification process.

The Institutional Base

The victory of the rebel army and the revolutionary forces laid the foundation for a series of actions that helped dismantle the forms of economic domination and political repression inherent in the neocolonial model and create the structures, legal forms, and other features required to stabilize the state institutions through which the people were to exercise democracy. In January 1959 the groundwork was laid for the establishment of the popular political system for which José Martí had fought. All that was left of the old apparatus of political power was part of the judicial system and certain offices with economic and administrative functions. The nation's traditional political parties crumbled, and the dominant antipopular trade union leadership was dissolved. The rebel army became the core around which Cuban society's new political system was created.[1]

The new state wasted no time in demonstrating that for it democracy was neither an incidental feature to be only formally applied nor an empty abstraction. The reclaiming of the nation's wealth from the hands of a minority for the benefit of the people as a whole, the elimination of unemployment and the creation of jobs, the eradication of poverty and illiteracy, the expansion of medical care and hospital services, and provision for the aged were all direct expressions of the essentially democratic roots of the revolutionary state.

With the triumph of the revolution, the bourgeoisie, opposed to the fundamental transformations entailed by the policy of social equity, deserted the nation, and this resulted in the dismemberment of the social base of the old political parties that had been in the service of oppression. Thus, the democracy that took hold acquired a new dimension; it was incorporated into social life, promoting both change in institutions and real access to them. Linked with this was a change in individual values that contributed to its consolidation. The events of this period can only be understood as a sociopolitical process that brought people into increasingly active political life. This was one of the keys to the success of the new system and to the viability of its early popular policies aimed at a rapid redistribution of income and an increase in the standard of living (on the latter, see Rodríguez and Carriazo, 1987).

The first steps of the new leadership were aimed at seeking plausible forms for the free exercise of national sovereignty. The dissolution of the traditional army eliminated the principal point of support that might have been used by the classes displaced from power and their main ally, the U.S. government, for action against the new revolutionary authorities. This made possible the gradual development of the bases for institutionalization of the revolution. In this early period some elements of the old system, such as the Ministry of the Treasury, were briefly preserved. The most effective tool used by the revolutionary government was the almost plebiscitary consultations on a series of new laws that substantially modified the configuration and exercise of power and the political life of the nation. The new role of the Central de Trabajadores de Cuba after the definitive victory of the revolutionary line within it and the rapid establishment of the most important mass organizations contributed to the creation of a truly socialist democracy.

Among the most important obstacles to the development of the newly created structures was the novelty of their conflict with the influence of the United States, which in the eyes of some had become customary and inevitable. Another was the relative lack of training in administration and experience in state matters on the part of the sectors that had historically been excluded from politics. With the social improvements and cultural advances initiated by the revolution, individuals eventually became better equipped for direct participation in political affairs. The 1961 literacy campaign opened up the possibility for a universalization of knowledge, and this was not an isolated case. Other very important developments included the creation of new jobs for teachers, the reorganization of education on the basis of different principles and goals, and the substantial broadening of access to sources of technical information and know-how. The key to the progress achieved in these three decades is without a doubt the adoption of a participatory method. The country was soon dotted with classrooms and laboratories, and effective concepts were applied to the university.[2] The revolutionary measures, the vigorous legislation in favor of the people (including the granting of access to recreational facilities that had belonged to the elite), and the increasing access to education and culture gradually shaped a citizenry capable of conscientious participation in the nation's social and political process, which in turn continued to motivate it to such participation.

Understandably, the difficult conditions created by the sharp confrontation with internal counterrevolution and imperialist activities precluded the creation of representative state institutions through traditional elections. The revolution was going through a crucial stage, and construction prevailed over institutionalization even though the leadership was aware of the need for the latter from the first. Among the other reasons representative institutions were not created from the very beginning of the revolution were the concern of the political vanguard with the solution of immediate problems, the feeling that the party should be organized first, and the belief that the development of mass organizations was a necessary preliminary step. Also important were the popular distaste for the so-called representative democracy of the past, insufficient understanding of the importance of these institutions, and a preoccupation with the economic development without which any institutionalization would have been extremely fragile.

The national independence that had finally been won and the many social demands advanced by the revolution had a decisive impact on the popular inertia originating in large part from an understandable lack of faith in the corrupt rulers with which the republic had been saddled. People began to become part of the social order, participants in the revolutionary state. Elections had traditionally been an arena for political intrigue, and for this reason they tended to be seen as a way of legitimating unhealthy administrations. Because people fully identified with the leadership of the revolution, they did not raise the issue of elections as a formula or premise for democracy, looking instead to the social and economic transformations that they felt were more urgently needed and that were being realized in the agrarian reform law, the urban reform law, the nationalizations, and so on. Experience proved that the transitional forms that characterized this period were sufficient to channel the social dynamic unleashed by the changing situation.

In the early period, the strategy for developing the country was expressed in the implementation of laws whose effect was an integral part of the effort to structure society on a new basis. The first agrarian reform law, enacted on May 17, 1959, was a decisive first step in reordering relations in the countryside. Later came the creation of the Asociación Nacional de Agricultores Pequeños (National Association of Small Farmers, ANAP), which brought together peasants who owned plots of land within the size limits established by the law. The unifying effect of the ANAP was a significant contribution to the implementation of the agrarian program of the revolution.

Other mass organizations, such as the Comités de Defensa de la Revolución, the Federación de Mujeres Cubanas, and the united front of youth originally called the Asociación de Jovenes Rebeldes (Young Rebels' Association), served as channels for the growing political mobilization. They were joined by student organizations—the Federación Estudiantil Universitaria (University Students' Federation, FEU), with its strong tradition of struggle among university students, and the Organización de Pioneros "José Martí" (José Martí Pioneers' Organization), the successor of the early Unión de Pioneros Rebeldes (Union of Rebel Pioneers).[3]

The conditions prevailing in this provisional period gave rise to the systematic use of forms of direct democracy whereby proposals for dealing with social, economic, and political problems of great interest to society were subjected to discussion and approval. The National Assembly of the Cuban people convened on September 2, 1960, and became the genesis of a parliament whose proceedings led to the analysis and eventual approval of the First and Second Declarations of Havana. The most important revolutionary law was certainly the one that gave legal form to the country's sovereignty and restored the 1940 constitution as the basic law of the Cuban state. The experience of countries such as the United States suggested that a series of laws could be added as amendments of specific aspects of the 1940 document in which change was needed. These modifications were adopted by popular vote and ratified in the First Declaration of Havana. From the moment this declaration was approved it became part of the Cuban constitution, which remained in force until in 1976 the socialist constitution was approved.

At the same time, there was systematic unmediated contact between the main leaders of the revolution and the masses, even if its particular forms were not always based on the legislation developed during those years. Consultation of the people through the trade unions, the CDRs, and the women's and youth organizations also made it possible to gather opinions and recommendations, and therefore the decisions made by the revolutionary leadership took on a national character not only because of their effects but because they were based upon knowledge of the interests of all sectors of the country. The effectiveness of popular participation can also be seen at another level, related to the crucial aspect of the first decade of the revolution: the successful defense of the nation's sovereignty. The incorporation of the masses into social and political life was also manifested in the solution of complex problems of production and other spheres under the pressure of circumstances created mainly by the absence of cadres specifically suited for given tasks.[4]

Along with the state institutions that were established there was another, no less important, vehicle—the production assembly. It brought together the workers of a given factory to exchange opinions on the tasks of their sector of the economy. These assemblies had considerable influence upon the factories and upon those who had administrative responsibilities; they provided training in the effective control of production.[5]

Certainly these early stages of institutionalization had their limitations. Popular participation required broader opportunities than were offered by the instruments of the state and continual revision on the basis of a clearer separation of the tasks of the political and the mass organizations.[6] By the end of the 1960s the latter's role had weakened, if not in numbers then in impact, and an important premise of the new institutionalization was the strengthening of these organizations and the clarification of their functions. Among the new organizational forms created by the revolution was the Junta de Coordinación, Ejecución e Inspección (Council for Coordination, Execution, and Inspection, JUCEI), which had the attributes of a local political authority and a special state apparatus for coordination and inspection at the local or provincial level (although lacking executive power in the economic field).[7] It functioned from 1961 until September 1965 and in October of that year was succeeded by Poder Local (Local Power)—an indication of the continuing interest in improving the mechanisms of the state and making them more responsive.

Of particular importance were the advances in organizational unity of the revolutionary forces under a single political leadership. There was a fusion of the various existing organizations, each contributing cadres with the experience and commitment that they had acquired. The first results of this process were the Organizaciones Revolucionarias Integradas (Integrated Revolutionary Organizations) and the Partido Unido de la Revolución Socialista (United Party of the Socialist Revolution). Left behind at this point was an era of mistaken concepts and erroneous methods that had cost the party its essential link to the masses and distorted its exercise of democratic centralism. The localized phenomenon known as the "microfaction"—a small group that attempted to establish a political line behind the party—also became a thing of the past. A central committee was formed in October 1965, and the decision was made to adopt the name Partido Comunista de Cuba. This was the culmination of a process of reconstruction in which diverse forces were brought together in a single body—the realization of a long-held goal of the Cuban revolutionaries.

It was basically after 1970 that this period was subjected to detailed analysis with the purpose of learning from experience. At the August 1970 meeting of the political bureau and secretariat of the party, systematic analysis was begun of the institutional projects that might be adopted in the future. This process was accelerated from 1972 on because of the maturation of conditions that made it unavoidable: economic recovery, the increased strength of the mass organizations, the experience gained through the previous exercise of leadership, and the existence of cadres capable of carrying out the tasks of a reorganization of the state. Up to this point, the completion of the elements of the state had been subordinated, as not a vital task, to the struggle for survival. Once the conditions for it had been created, the realization of new institutional forms for the Cuban state was urgent. The goal was to make popular participation more regular, more effective, and more mature. The process of institutionalization also included the correction of actions by state institutions in a context favorable to the operation of broader democratic mechanisms and the reduction of the incidence of spontaneous individual and social political activity.

The restructuring of the Council of Ministers and the creation of its executive committee took place at the end of 1972. The entire party apparatus was modified in 1973 and its role and responsibilities delimited. The judicial system was reorganized, and the CTC held a thirteenth congress that helped make its impact on society more effective. Preparations for the pilot project of Poder Popular, in the province of Matanzas, began at the end of 1973. Two events were of particular significance in this context: the first congress of the Partido Comunista de Cuba in 1975 and the establishment of Poder Popular on a national scale in December of the same year.

Mass Participation

The inauguration of Poder Popular—the institutionalized participation of the masses in state administration in general rather than just in the election of their representatives—marked a second stage in the development of political leadership in Cuba. The favorable effects of the legacy of the preceding years can be clearly seen in this process. In the first place, the many channels created early on were a stimulus to the participation of the masses and to their greater identification with social interests. In the second place, it continued to be common practice for the highest leadership to consult the masses, and this lent broad representativeness to its fundamental decisions. The dialogue between the people and their leaders gradually gave rise to a political culture that, though far from ideal, does place the individual at an advantage in terms of the ability to respond to the tensions and demands of the community, the workplace, or the labor or student group. The individual's contribution to the solution of social problems is reproduced many times over in collective action that liberates talents, remedies alienation, and links fragmented intentions in intense mass activity. The early, almost intuitive practice of sounding people out led Guevara to take special note of the nature of the interaction between Fidel and the people, which he likened to a dialogue between tuning forks (1985b:253).

Essential to the exercise of democracy is the strengthening of the climate of juridical and political liberty. The juridical framework was completed with the approval of the constitution, the culmination of a process of extensive popular participation. From February to November 1975, while the draft constitution was being analyzed and discussed, there were no fewer than 16,248 modifications, additions, and proposals.[8] The referendum held on February 15, 1976, to ratify the constitution was carried out through the free, direct, and secret vote of Cuban citizens sixteen years of age and older, and 98 percent of them took part.

Change in the system of social and individual values was registered in the development of new political-moral parameters and a greater commitment to mobilization. The revolution caused major transformations both in economics and in the juridical, political, and social spheres, and this was refracted with different degrees of intensity in each Cuban's individual perspective. The economic development achieved despite adverse circumstances led to a marked improvement in living conditions. The economy has grown at a rate of more than 4 percent per year; the generation of electricity has been multiplied by eight, the production of steel by sixteen, and the production of cement by more than five. Furthermore, freed of secular racial barriers and other obstacles such as discrimination against individuals because of their sex or their birth, people saw that their participation as political beings was being encouraged, attributes that in the past had been sine qua non for real influence in the life of the country having been stripped away. While under the democratic illusions of the past, discrepancies between the letter of the law and reality had been rife, socialism in Cuba had created its own means of correspondence between them as an expression of the harmonization of the interests of the citizen and those of society.

This is not simply presenting our truth in terms of the conceptual parameters and styles of argumentation and exposition that arouse such skepticism these days. It is difficult to respond effectively to criticism of Cuban democracy that is based on stereotypes whose possibilities have been completely exhausted; thus one is tempted to make the mistake of setting up an unfair balance between social achievements and individual freedoms in Cuba in an attempt to establish sterile comparisons with other situations.

The Single-Party Question

People not fully familiar with the Cuban experience often argue that democracy is impossible with a single party, but this argument hinges upon the presumed paradigms of a multiparty system. The existence of a single party in Cuba has juridical and political justification, and it is based on the particular historical trajectory of its struggle for independence. Under the banner of the unity of all revolutionaries in the struggle against colonialism and for national independence in the nineteenth century, José Martí, the founder of the Partido Revolucionario Cubano (Cuban Revolutionary Party), spoke of it as follows: "It was born as one, from all parts at once. And anyone, be he from within or without, who might think that it can be extinguished or disdained would be in error. What is the ambition of a group falls. What a people desires endures. The Cuban Revolutionary Party is the Cuban people" (Martí, 1975:366).

The unity of the revolutionary forces in a single party following the victory of the Cuban Revolution was the result of the fusion of three organizations that in their opposition to the Batista dictatorship were in fundamental agreement on the general principles of anti-imperialism and national and social liberation. In the course of the struggle they overcame their tactical differences and adopted those of the movement led by Fidel Castro. Thus, the forces of the Partido Socialista Popular (People's Socialist Party, PSP), the Marxist-Leninist party that had existed in Cuba since 1925, fused with those of the Movimiento 26 de Julio and the Directorio Revolucionario on the basis of Marxist-Leninist ideology and the ideas of José Martí under the leadership of Fidel.

From 1902, when the bourgeois republic was proclaimed, until 1958, the last year of the Batista dictatorship, all the republican multiparty system did in the country was to serve as a favorable environment for the worsening of social conflicts. It never resolved any of the problems affecting broad sectors of the nation. Because of this, along with the discredit that it earned as the struggle against tyranny unfolded, it had exhausted its potential. That the process of liberation that culminated in January 1959 found no support among the traditional parties has a historical explanation: These parties were linked or committed in some way to the Cuban and foreign bourgeoisie and were incapable of involving themselves in the imminent perspectives for development opened up by national liberation.

The existence of a single party is a result of history itself, the requirements of the building of socialism in Cuba, the special circumstances that for more than three decades have favored unity of action on the part of the Cuban people (the assaults of successive U.S. administrations, the persistent economic blockade of the island, and aggression via television), the adverse conditions resulting from the transition to development, and the impact of the current crisis of socialism. The party born of the revolution represents the legitimate interests of the broadest social sectors. It has led historic battles for the spread of development across the country as well as the confrontation with the powerful neighbor to the north. If the existence of several parties had been a prerequisite for the building of socialism we would have had to create such parties artificially, fragmenting our party's broad social base to the detriment of our essential cohesion. The unity factor, which has deep roots in Martí and Lenin, is identified with Cuban society's new goals and values and, above all, with its plural subject—an enriched synthesis of individuals who have come together consciously and freely to pool their talents and energies, adopting as their own the highest project for social well-being, socialism.

Under these conditions, mass democracy has improved and acquired special meaning, being the way of ensuring fruitful debate inside and outside the Party on the fundamental problems for which the Cuban revolutionaries must find solutions. The critical attitude that is increasingly developing within the Party and in the various social and mass organizations gains strength from the revolutionary positions taken by the majority of the population. In this regard, Fidel Castro has said, "The revolution has always had criticism and self-criticism. If one analyzes revolutionary processes, it is hard to find an example like that of the Cuban Revolution in the exercise of public criticism and self-criticism. . . . Under our conditions, the opposition must be the party itself, the revolutionary cadres themselves, each at their own level. And we practice it with all frankness and honesty" (Miná, 1988:189, 190).

There is a substantial difference between this and the opposition that exists under the banner of bourgeois democracy. In the latter both the parties in power and those not in power represent the interests of a minority of the nation, and in these circumstances opposition expresses the polarization of social forces. It presents its disagreements by proposing possible alternatives. It might well be asked, however, whether this type of system, in which the parties take turns in office, is not simply a matter of choosing between one bourgeois party and another, which in the last analysis allows only a vote for one or another sector of the ruling class.

The isolated groups that in Cuba demand the right to function as a political opposition have their social base in the United States. Inspired by the negative processes that are taking place in Eastern Europe and encouraged by imperialism, they take a position that is incompatible with the favorable results of our socialism and try to present it as being in the interests of all of society. This opposition is synonymous with counter-revolution, and it has always been and will remain proimperialist and antipatriotic.

The process of rectification of errors and negative tendencies launched in April 1986 and particularly the convocation of the fourth congress of the Party encourage thinking about ways of improving the structures of democracy. They encourage the search for solutions to problems, changes in the approach to socioeconomic goals, and democratic discussion in general within the Party and the revolution. At the same time they demand that steps be taken to correct the country's economic course and to overcome the imperfections in the work of various political and state sectors.

Rectification, far from being a passing thing or a return to the past, is a revitalization of the Cuban road to socialism—a full return to the method that made the revolution possible. It strengthens a style of work rooted in the daily commitment of the masses, in further stimulation of their creativity, in the optimal utilization of their potential—a democratic impulse that had diminished in the face of bureaucratization and dogmatic theoretical interpretation.

With regard to the latter, what was particularly harmful was the economistic tendency that prevailed until the mid-1980s, claiming, supposedly in the name of the country's economic prosperity, to promote the fulfillment of production and service goals with material incentives (themselves distorted) alone. This blocked the development of satisfactory work conduct, exalted indiscipline and lack of interest in social goals, and stimulated a lack of inventiveness and uncritical imitation of foreign experiments. No less harmful were such distortions as the ascendancy of technocratic conceptions, the proliferation of bureaucracy, and the development in some sectors of a commercialized and profit-oriented mentality. All this promoted inaction, conformism, parasitic tendencies, and corruption in society.

The process of rectification reaffirms the broad popular base of political power in Cuba. It creates a favorable atmosphere for the exchange of different points of view. It encourages the real (not illusory) participation of workers in the improvement of the forms and expressions of socialist democracy. It is backed by the political responsibility of the Party, which is conscientiously and carefully promoting it.

In Cuba, democratic centralism is the rule. The unconvinced minority has no choice but to accept the course decided upon collectively. This does not, of course, make the majority a depersonalized, manipulated mass, as the myth often propagated by those who are not partisans of socialism would have it, nor does it mean any uniformity of viewpoints within that majority. Individual idiosyncrasies alone preclude such uniformity. What there is no room for, however, is the unbridled individual desires that would interfere with the integration of all points of view. With democratic centralism the masses play the active leadership role and have the concrete, institutionalized power to make proposals and decisions. For example, elections of representatives to the organs of state power are decided from the bottom up by the masses: The majority of the members of the National Assembly (54.7 percent) are elected by the rank and file.

The highest authority is the people who do the electing, not those elected, and there is also the possibility of recall. When voters elect their representatives, they exercise power through them. Whereas elsewhere citizens exercise democracy in the periodic act of voting, in Cuba democracy is permanent in a number of ways. In the accountability assemblies (*asambleas de rendición de cuentas*) held twice a year, for example, delegates face those who have elected them and render an account of their activities. These assemblies have become a free and characteristic forum. Furthermore, there is participation even in the selection of candidates for election; the latter are not imposed by a party but nominated by the citizens of each district, and there can never be fewer than two nominees.

To this must be added the absence of demagogic election campaigns and attempts to affect the political or social representativeness of the results in one way or another. The electoral law establishes equal conditions for all candidates. Their photographs and biographies are posted in public places thirty days before the election so that their basic data can be known. An obvious advantage of this effective method is that a vote for a candidate is based not on how much money he has or some other factor that has nothing to do with democracy but on his own virtues— his ability to represent those who choose him, the behavior that has earned him the voters' trust. Elections themselves are marked by their fairness and honesty, in contrast to the corruption and dirty politics that were the norm in the past.

Finally, Poder Popular functions on the principle of collective leadership. This does not mean that there is no freedom of discussion; on the contrary, it is encouraged.

The heterogeneity and variation in present-day Cuban society are expressed in the composition of state institutions; they are an indicator of the political culture that has developed in Cuban society. Some figures related to this can be drawn from the results of the 1989 elections. Of the delegates at the national level, 14.8 percent are black and 19.1 percent are mestizo; these two groups together make up 34 percent of the country's population. Twenty-two percent of the delegates are youth, and 16.7 percent are women (Castro, 1987:100). The makeup of the National Assembly over time reflects the social composition of the nation. Ethnic groups, for example, are fully represented, as blacks and mestizos make up 36 percent. The proportion of women and youth has grown to 34.9 percent. Workers directly linked to production and services make up 41.6 percent. Fifty-six percent are university graduates, which speaks well for the country's educational achievements and the feeling of voters that they are better represented (Castro, 1987:100). One strong indicator of real popular participation and representativeness is the fact that there is one delegate for every 508 inhabitants, and another is the fact that the number of districts has risen from 10,725 in 1976 to 14,247 in 1989.

The thoroughness of the country's democratic system is apparent in the functioning of the accountability process. In each such process voters present some one hundred thousand proposals or issues, of which about half are resolved concretely and directly. Others can be resolved only through measures that do not always involve financing but rather call for improvement on the part of the people in charge and the leadership. It should not be overlooked that the issues raised by the voters represent substantially different levels on the scale of social development. Thus, the satisfaction of one set of needs immediately creates new expectations. At the same time, the demands vary in their content. For example, previously in the public health sector there were requests for the establishment of certain medical services and specialized clinics. Once these demands were met, the issues raised had more to do with the quality of the services received.

All of this does not mean that democracy in Cuba is a finished product. It is of course subject to constant revision and is affected as much by historical circumstances as by deviations having to do with facts of consciousness. The convocation of the fourth Party congress points to the need to review the functioning of our socialist democracy, which includes both the leadership of state institutions, government, and administration and the work, structure, and approach of the Unión de Jóvenes Comunistas and the mass and social organizations, with the aim of reaffirming what is positive and freeing them of formalism and other shortcomings. The establishment of more mature state structures ensures their more structured connection with the masses, but the fulfillment of democracy cannot depend upon mechanisms alone. Furthermore, the mechanisms themselves are subject to improvement. The convocation makes explicit reference to the need to discuss the functioning of Poder Popular.

Even before the process of rectification was in full swing, the Party's program included guidelines for the improvement of Cuba's democratic system. There was a clear understanding on the highest levels of the leadership that popular participation in the nation's various social arenas is essential to the foundations of democracy in Cuba and that if democracy is to be fully exercised there must be improvement at all levels of its functioning. Deficiencies in the functioning of democracy are recognized first of all by Cubans themselves. There may still be certain symptoms of formalism, administrative authoritarianism, mechanical following of orders, and prefabricated solutions, but rectification is seen as the way of eradicating the conjunctural deviations, eliminating mistaken conceptions and negative methods of operation, improving the human component, and expanding human potential.

Popular participation in Cuba is not limited to Poder Popular; it extends to all aspects of the society's political system. Precisely what Fidel Castro has called a "mass formula," reclaimed and reinvigorated by the rectification process, is at work as a unifying force in the correction of the path to socialism. An important premise is the ensured participation of the people, as a manifestation of broad democratization, in the search for solutions to social problems that harmonize real material possibilities and the maturity of the human factor. This is the full meaning of a context that highlights the social subject as the true leadership in increasing the effectiveness of the structures created.

Notes

1. Embryonic organs of the new power appeared during the insurrectional period (Fernández Ríos, 1985); the decrees issued from the Sierra Maestra, especially Law No. 2 of October 10, 1958 (political disenfranchisement of electoral candidates), and Law No. 3 of that same year (agrarian reform), are important in understanding this process (Gobierno Provisional de la República, 1959).

2. The First National Congress of Education and Culture in April 1971 provided an opportunity for communication among participants on important aspects of education and culture.

3. A few statistics illustrate the popular participation of that period. With regard to women, for example, in January 1961 the FMC was still in the process of being organized but already had 17,000 members; by the following year membership had risen to 239,342. The Federación Estudiantil de la Enseñanza Media (Federation of Secondary-Level Students, FEEM), founded on December 6, 1970, is the most recent of the mass organizations, bringing together preuniversity students and those in schools of an equivalent level.

4. Issues related to the education of cadres and their suitability are extensively discussed in the works of Ernesto Che Guevara (see 1985b).

5. After 1970 a change took place in the functioning of these assemblies with a view to increasing workers' participation in the economic management of the country (see Harnecker, 1979).

6. For example, because of the specific circumstances of this period the ANAP had to take on a series of administrative tasks, which in practice it continued to carry out until its seventh congress in 1987 (Lugo Fonte, 1989).

7. The JUCEI included revolutionary organizations as well as delegates of the administrative bodies. Its role was to coordinate these groups and promote the full utilization of the country's productive potential at the local level (Guevara, 1985a).

8. A decisive step was taken during the first congress of the PCC, where there was discussion of the main tasks that had to be carried out through December 1978 in order to move ahead with the application of the new political-administrative divisions and the constitution of the organs of Poder Popular (PCC, 1975).

References

Castro, Fidel. 1987. "Intervención en la clausura de la sesión constitutiva de la III Legislatura de la Asamblea Nacional de Poder Popular." *Cuba Socialista* (25): 98–104.

Fernández Ríos, Olga. 1985. "El ejército rebelde y la dictadura democrático-revolucionaria de las masas populares." *Revista Cubana de Ciencias Sociales* 7 (January–April).

Gobierno Provisional de la República. 1959. *Ley fundamental de la república.* Havana: Lex.

Guevara, Ernesto Che. 1985a. "Discusión colectiva: decisión y responsabilidad únicas," in *Escritos y discursos,* vol. 5. Havana: Ciencias Sociales.

———. 1985b. "El cuadro, columna vertebral de la revolución," in *Escritos y discursos,* vol. 6. Havana: Ciencias Sociales.

Harnecker, Marta. 1979. *Cuba: Los protagonistas de un nuevo poder.* Havana: Ciencias Sociales.

Lugo Fonte, Orlando. 1989. "La ANAP: sus principales tareas." *Cuba Socialista* 39 (May–June):1–14.

Martí, José. 1975. "El partido revolucionario cubano," in *Obras completas,* vol. 6. Havana: Ciencias Sociales.

Miná, Gianni. 1988. *Un encuentro con Fidel.* Havana: Oficina de Publicaciones del Consejo de Estado.

PCC (Partido Comunista de Cuba). 1975. *Informe central al Primer Congreso.* Havana: DOR del Comité Central.

Rodríguez, José Luis, and George Carriazo. 1987. *Erradicación de la pobreza en Cuba.* Havana: Ciencias Sociales.

5

Cuban Socialism: Prospects and Challenges

Fernando Martínez Heredia

Translated by Janell Pierce

The process of socialist reinforcement initiated in Cuba in 1986 has taken the form of an indigenous political critique of measures adopted immediately following the revolution that proved damaging to the effective development of socialism. This critique is an attempt to rectify errors and to pursue the lasting, well-planned progress—socialist progress inspired by communism—of all of society. The reforms that have been taking place in the European socialist countries and their international consequences have affected this rectification, making it especially difficult to understand Cuban reality and the Cuban agenda without taking them into account.

Concern was expressed during 1989 over whether Cuba might remain isolated, fettered to an obsolete orthodoxy, while elsewhere socialism was pursuing efficiency and democracy through the liberalization of its political and economic institutions. Questions were raised about the possible response of the leadership to the idea of similar internal reforms, the effect on the economy of alteration of Cuba's ties to the Soviet Union, the consequences of détente among the major powers for Cuba's anti-imperialist stance, and the likelihood of internal struggles for the continuing leadership of the revolution or of outbreaks of popular discontent. In order not to depend on anecdotes and superficialities—or be at the mercy of those who dominate the formation of public opinion—we must move onto more substantial ground, specifically, the principal characteristics and predictable tendencies of Cuban socialism. Here we will find what we need to reformulate these questions, add others, and perhaps even obtain some answers.

It is ironic that Latin America's most exciting social experiment is so rarely the object of scholarly study and knowledge; instead, comments are made that try to be to the point but create an abstract or illusory image of Cuba in relation to the ideas emerging from the Eastern European countries and urge emulation of the "democratization" of those countries—so dissimilar even among themselves—to avoid a change on the Romanian model. Notably absent in the majority of these appraisals is any reference to the position of Cuba in Latin America, its condition as a small, underdeveloped, militant Third World country, the mortal contradiction between North American imperialism and Cuba's past, its present, and its national objectives, or the material and spiritual realities at the core of the Cuban Revolution. We Cubans are in part responsible for this situation because of our shortcomings in offering and disseminating information, our defensiveness, and the vicissitudes of our social thought. The fact that powerful forces are operating against us is well known, but this should serve as an incentive to overcome these deficiencies.

Freedom, Socialism, and Democracy in Cuba

The Cuban system is socialist not because of any theoretical imperative but because the revolutionary government from its inception found socialism the most viable means for permanently freeing Cuba from foreign domination and guaranteeing its sovereignty and self-determination, mobilizing, educating, and organizing the popular forces in the midst of tremendous anticapitalist changes that entailed wrenching changes for the people themselves, and restructuring from the ground up the means of production and the reproduction of the forms of social life, political power, and the body of prevailing ideas and beliefs so that the economy, political power, and ideology would remain in the hands and at the service of the majority.

Cuba is a small island in the Caribbean, at the foot of the United States, that has been colonized and neocolonized, its wealth going to support the development of the world capitalist centers—a major provider of raw materials and recipient of industrial products and capital whose population, production, commerce, and social life are all at the mercy of outside forces. But it is also a nation with its own profile, a nation that, at the cost of extraordinary struggles, has managed to achieve independence and the ideal of national liberation. It is a nation that has incorporated democratic ideals and behavior since the beginning of its wars of independence more than a century ago and that gave birth to the first political party in the world founded to secure national independence through armed struggle and its creator, José Martí. Later, as the first neocolony of the United States, it experienced a rich history of class struggle and another revolution in the 1930s that modified the system of domination. A clear link was identified between anti-imperialism, the tradition of armed struggle, and socialist ideas. A model of political and ideological reformism was developed, but it was based on the superexploitation of the worker and the scandalous misery of the masses—all of which led to a battle to the death between dictatorship and revolution.

Cuba is still characterized by an element of underdevelopment in its international economic relations, since it must sell its principal and primary products abroad and is vulnerable to external influences in finance, technology, and equipment and tangible inputs. It dramatically altered the direction of its economic relations in the face of the illegal and permanent blockade imposed by the United States, securing its freedom by means of its association with the socialist countries. The free arms and vast political support of the Soviet Union and its economic assistance and commercial partnership were extremely important to the Cuban process. The just economic relations—relations not based on the profit standard—to which the two countries agreed have been very beneficial to our economy and have been a practical example of what socialism can achieve in terms of a new type of equitable international relationship between underdeveloped and developed countries.

In liberated underdeveloped countries it is especially easy to see the twofold difficulty that confronts a socialist transition. First, the persistence of mercantile relations on a national and an international scale tends to perpetuate national and individual roles based on profit, advantage, selfishness, individualism, position in the market economy, and the accompanying attitudes concerning production, distribution, consumption, and power. Second, individuals and institutions find themselves incapable, especially given the relative lack of technological development, of changing the destructive pattern of preexisting neocolonial capitalism that hinders or even obstructs socialist development. At the same time, over the past forty or fifty years the realm of revolutionary ideas and acts of liberation has expanded and gained strength more than that of the general development of socialism worldwide, and this imbalance has greatly limited the role of internationalism in socialist theory and practice. Through its ability to undermine the limitations and difficulties that arise for national socialist projects, internationalism allows countries to raise their socialist and human development far beyond what a purely national context would allow. A crucial aspect, then, is the creation of a cultural focus essentially opposed to capitalism that is capable of attracting both the sentiment and the interest of individuals and communities. Without this ongoing process of total cultural change, there will be no socialism.

Socialism is, above all, political and ideological power and a revolutionary plan to improve society. From the beginning it has been considered heretical because it has sought to do what common sense and organized theory deemed impossible. Fidel said in 1969 that whereas Marx conceived of socialism as a result of development, for the contemporary underdeveloped world socialism was a condition of development. Che Guevara had written in his guerrilla diary in Bolivia two years earlier that the meaning of the 26th of July was rebellion against the oligarchy and against revolutionary dogma. Socialism is therefore a process of successive upheavals not only in the economy, politics, and ideology but in conscious and organized action. It is a process premised on unleashing the power of the people, who learn how to change themselves along with their circumstances. Revolutions within the revolution demand creativity and unity with respect to principles and organization and broad and growing participation. In other words, they must become a gigantic school through which people learn to direct social processes. Socialism is not constructed spontaneously, nor is it something that can be bestowed.

The revolutionary origin of the Cuban government has been decisive in its legitimation. The victory of the people's army and the tremendous struggles that followed thoroughly destroyed and discredited the previous system. Revolutionary accomplishments left prior illusions far behind and overcame mistakes and misfortunes. In the process the foundations of Cuban socialism were erected and new bonds of solidarity formed between the people, their communities, and the nation. The continued legitimation of the revolution has in many fundamental ways been shaped by the political behavior of the masses. The power of the state is not only popular in origin but identified as the appropriate means for producing change, defending the revolution, and guaranteeing popular victories, progress, and the continuation of the regime. In spite of its tenacious bureaucratization, shortcomings in the service sector, and a variety of mistakes, Cubans' experience with this powerful state has, on balance, been positive, and they view the state's power as belonging to them. Endowed not only with an impressive legal system that ensures the security of its citizens and community institutions but also with the most democratic local power on the continent—Poder Popular, in force since 1976—the Cuban state continues to be valued by the great majority of the population despite numerous criticisms of its very real and serious deficiencies.

The one-party system is not, any more than was the triumph of the revolution, a result of the history of the international communist movement but a consequence of the unity achieved by the revolutionaries and the rest of the population after divisive struggle. This unity still characterizes Cuban politics and is one of the major successes of the revolution. It is representative of the Party, in which division, history, ideals, and revolutionary plans all come together. Enlisting its members on the basis of selectivity and excellence recognized by the labor collectives, it has shared ideological principles and strong discipline. Its power rests, above all, in its vast moral authority. Through its prestige and influence and through the leadership functions assigned to it, it represents a political counterbalance to the state and a participatory opportunity for its half-million members.

I will not offer a full account of the social accomplishments of Cuban socialism, but I would be remiss in failing to credit it with full employment over two decades, increasing family incomes, vast social security benefits, fully covered costs of education and health care, major advances in the quality of life, an infant mortality rate of 11.1 per thousand, a life expectancy of almost seventy-five years (1989), genuine equality in basic services, a sharp increase in social solidarity, a discrediting of prestige based on property and initiative motivated by personal profit, a sharp reduction in disparity of income, extraordinary social mobility, and so forth. Major political policies—including that of internationalism—have recognized these social achievements as the outcome of the concerted efforts and sacrifices of all of the people and as inherent in the nature of the socialist regime. Among the characteristics of socialism in Cuba that clearly differentiate it from that of modern Eastern Europe are radical social changes in the way of life and in the meaning of life, complete national independence, sovereignty, national unity, national pride, feelings of belonging to a large community of people and solidarity with them, popular government, and political education and behavior.

The Economy: Strengths and Weaknesses

The Cuban economy grew at an annual rate of 4.8 percent between 1959 and 1985 (based on constant 1965 prices), and labor productivity rose 2.9 percent. Gross investment in that period was 47,453.6 million pesos, and acreage under cultivation rose from 2 million to 3.8 million hectares. Between 1961 and 1981 the role of primary activities in the gross national product (GNP) went from 18.2 to 12.9 percent, while industrial activities rose from 31.8 to 46.4 percent; the average rate of growth in raw agricultural production from 1962 to 1983, at constant prices, was 2.9 annually, while that in industrial production was 5.0. Meanwhile, income distribution was transformed: The poorest 40 percent of the population received 6.5 percent in 1953 and 26 percent in 1986; the share of the wealthiest 10 percent declined from 38.8 percent to 20.1 percent. The GNP per capita increased 3.1 percent per year between 1960 and 1985, whereas the GNP for the rest of Latin America increased only 1.8 percent in the same period (see Rodríguez, 1988; n.d.:18; Brundenius, 1985; Zimbalist and Brundenius, 1989:14, 28).

This period includes the first decade of enormous transformation in social relations and its painful consequences (including the emigration of a portion of our skilled labor) and the major reorientation from a neo-colonial economy to an international one that resulted in the U.S. blockade. Moreover, tremendous effort continued to have to be expended on defense, and even today this claims many thousands of our most qualified young people as well as enormous resources. Never before in the Americas has there been such a redistribution of social wealth, and it has been accomplished not by sacrificing part of the population but by eliminating luxury consumer items and certain nonbasic ones. The formidable national effort directed toward the introduction and development of the socialist economy has enjoyed total and ongoing support, support that has been essential given that the policies of the regime include arming the people. In my opinion, the massive political and ideological acceptance of the economic strategy of the revolution has been decisive in defeating capitalism in Cuba and legitimating the socialist model.

For example, the sugar industry went from an average production of 5.6 million metric tons between 1951 and 1959 to 7.65 million metric tons per year between 1981 and 1989 (Moreno Fraginales, 1978:47–48; CEE, various years; *Granma,* June 2, 1989), and these recent harvests have been made with only 20 percent of the number of farm workers employed three decades ago; mechanization, however, reached 68 percent, and the price of sugarcane increased 100 percent. There is no comparison between the conditions that existed for those who slaved under the old system and today's levels of compensation, services, and culture. In order to achieve these results it was necessary to invest enormous resources in restoring, expanding, and modernizing old factories, introducing mechanization, resolving complex chemical engineering problems, inventing and producing new harvesters, establishing centers for storing and cleaning the cane, watering, fertilizing, training tens of thousands of technicians and cadres, and so forth.

The production of citrus illustrates the importance to socialism of the economic benefits of education. A large part of the half-million scholarship recipients over the past decade have fulfilled their daily quota of physical work in this industry, and the result has been production that has increased sixfold over 1970, reaching one million metric tons.

With these accomplishments in mind, it is easier to comprehend the formidable challenges that Cuba has had to face in its advance toward a socialist economy. The accelerated autonomous development predicted in the 1960s proved impossible, as did the liberation of other Latin American countries that would have paved the way for the beginning of regional integration. Upon joining the Council for Mutual Economic Assistance (CMEA) in 1972, Cuba pointed to its apparent lack of integration and the underdeveloped and vulnerable character of its international position not only as a provider of raw materials but also in commercial, technological, and financial areas. These weaknesses continue to provide the incentive for aggression on the part of present-day imperialists. Yet, despite its prolonged political stability, important natural resources, advanced levels of health care (both technological and cultural), good roads, and so forth, Cuba has not proven attractive to investors.

The export of sugar continues to be the main source of revenue (around 75 percent of the total), but the advances made in the use of sugar derivatives have not led to significant new production. Reserves of nickel and iron (ranked among the best in the world) have not produced great profit, nor have the thirty years of hard work and success in extracting cobalt produced significant results. Production of steel is low. Cuba does not manufacture electric motors, and the automotive industry is still young. Only one-sixth of Cuba's imports are from capitalist countries, but these are very significant for production and services, involving such things as inputs, technology, and equipment. Furthermore, Cuba has not advanced sufficiently in the export of goods and services to the capitalist world or in the replacement of imports from it.

Cuban-Soviet trade increased from 50 percent of Cuba's total commerce between 1965 and 1975 to 60 percent in 1980 and 70.6 percent in 1985. The Soviet Union extended credit to cover deficits (6.8 billion pesos between 1959 and 1985) and granted favorable terms of exchange that ensured stability of activity and, to an appreciable extent, the possibility of Cuban economic planning in the 1970s. Soviet technical assistance, the training of specialists, and loans for development were very important in numerous areas of the Cuban economy, above all in industry. According to Soviet sources, Cuba provided 33–50 percent of the sugar and more than 40 percent of the citrus consumed in the Soviet Union, plus valuable nickel and cobalt and other products. The Soviet Union in return supplied fuels, machinery, equipment and spare parts, raw materials and metals, electrical household appliances, and foodstuffs. Economic relations with the Soviet Union have been the most extensive, integrated, and important that Cuba has maintained with any country in the past twenty-five years; international trade with other countries of the Eastern bloc amounted to 12.6 percent of Cuba's total (CEE, 1987a; 1987b:415–416; Rodríguez, 1986:7–33; Kamorin, 1989).

In recent years the economic situation in Cuba has in many respects been unfavorable. The worsening of droughts during the 1980s adversely affected cane production to the extent that Cuba has been forced since

1987 to purchase a million tons of sugar annually in order to fulfill its trade commitments with the European socialist countries. The losses resulting from a deterioration in the terms of exchange that have been noticeable in the world capitalist markets have also had their impact on trade relations between the socialist countries. With hardly any new loans extended, Cuba's foreign debt to the capitalist countries increased from $4,985,000,000 in 1986 to $6,450,000,000 by December 31, 1988, and the devaluations in the dollar hurt Cuba by inflating the currency of its creditors. Cuba's situation with respect to foreign exchange has been difficult throughout the revolutionary period. In the face of a growing negative trade balance and a lack of foreign currency, a strict austerity policy of reduced imports had to be enforced; high interest rates also had a negative effect upon the growth of the economy. In 1987 the gross social product (GSP) fell to 96.1 percent of that in 1986; the recovery achieved in 1988, at 102.5 percent of the GSP of 1987 (based on 1981 cost of production), represents in real terms only 60 percent of the decrease experienced in 1986–1987 (Banco Nacional de Cuba, 1989; CEE, 1988:101).

The initiatives required by these adverse circumstances must take into account the profound changes that have taken place in Eastern Europe as well as the process of Cuban rectification, which, though fully concerned with the economy, is not in any way restricted to it. These initiatives must therefore be part of an economic approach determined by an overall general strategy. Discussion of this subject is just beginning to unfold, and therefore I want to emphasize the speculative and in some cases hypothetical nature of what follows even though I consider all its appraisals well-founded.

The difficulties in economic relations with socialist Europe in recent years were greatly magnified in 1989. Although the Soviet leaders expressed a desire to maintain the nature and the extent of their economic ties with Cuba, the process under way in the Soviet Union was already being felt in Cuba in the form of serious delays in deliveries of goods needed for production, services, and the consumer market (for example, shipments of petroleum and wheat [see Fidel's speeches in *Granma*, July 26 and 28, 1990, and Castro, 1990]). At the same time, there were those in the Soviet Union who opposed the continuation of the system of bilateral relations. It is difficult to predict the potential impacts of all this on the functioning and planning of the Cuban economy, which has been to a large extent dependent on Soviet technology and parts for its industrial infrastructure as well as significant consumer products. The Soviet Union has also provided a market for the sale of a number of Cuban products.

The transformation of the CMEA, a topic on the agenda of its forty-fifth assembly (January 1990), reflects the changes in direction being made by European member countries—several of which are already leaning toward market economies and integration into the world capitalist economy. It is unlikely that the governing principles of the organization will remain unchanged. Both in its position as a member country and in its bilateral relations (which I consider to have always been decisive in the case of the CMEA), Cuba faces the uncertainty of not knowing how much will change and how much will turn out to be contrary to its interests. In the past, its trade with some of these countries has been of considerable importance.

The crisis of socialism in Europe is a fact, and its ideological implications extend to all parts of the world. Many critics contend that this crisis demonstrates that socialism "in general" is a historical mistake or a failed experiment; others allege that the proper path for socialism is the freeing of market mechanisms in the economy and the institution in the political realm of an open, multiparty system that would eliminate the leading role of communist parties in the political and civil sphere. Because the ideology of abstract democracy embraces the nomenclature of "democratization," at the present stage of these countries socialism becomes synonymous with a lack of democracy. The realities under way in Eastern Europe complicate the situation and challenge the position of Cuban socialism; the beliefs that they promote are too different from our own.

More Problems, More Rectification, More Socialism

The process of rectification of mistakes and negative tendencies in Cuba's revolutionary process has coincided with the adverse economic situation and the profound crisis of so-called real socialism. Tensions and contradictions have been magnified by the extraordinary moral and political forces, by the successes already realized by society in the new way of living and in the values that this promotes, and by the assortment of old and new social ills that the rectification is aimed at eliminating. After the initial stage in which a transitional socialist society was created and strengthened among us, and in the face of limits on the rate of economic development and the lack of revolutionary victories in America to which I have referred, a second stage comprising the first half of the 1970s can be identified in which the so-called errors of idealism (mainly the desire to advance too rapidly) of the previous phase were confronted. Next in importance to a sound understanding of the need to reorganize the economy and social and political institutions and to create an institutional framework capable of guaranteeing the stability of the advances and not impeding future revolutionary progress, a widespread, uncritical acceptance of both the experience and the dominant ideology of the European socialist countries—reinforced by its so-called Marxist-Leninist scientificness—was also seen. This acceptance was accompanied by an underestimation of important elements of the first phase, which resulted in the abandonment of independent thought and the neglect of the practical search for solutions in the complex matter of the socialist transition.

The belief that socialism could be constructed spontaneously by combining mercantile mechanisms and individualist motivations took hold among us. It was supposed that a mercantile structure could exist without capitalism under the tutelage of the socialist state until such time as "development" or a "material base" could pull behind it all the other aspects of society. The system of economic direction employed between the first and the third congresses of the Partido Comunista de Cuba (1975–1986) was a response to an economic policy inspired by that belief. It was based on a strategy that emphasized monetary-commercial relations while maintaining a heavily centralized economy, and it was characterized by an odd combination of technocratic leadership, bureaucratism, mercantilism, misinformation, formalized relations, and centralized planning. State institutionalization reinforced the illusion that the mechanisms introduced would form an almost perfect framework.

The list of the consequences of underdeveloped mercantilism is vast. Among other shortcomings it includes inefficiency, loss of control, a tendency toward uncritical conformity reinforced by the orientation of the training received by cadres and technicians, the squandering of resources, the inordinate appeal to individual material interest, economic activity based on profit and measured by profitability, lack of interest in social needs, privileges and advantages, the silencing of criticism, and the private commercialization of numerous products and services. Achievements measured in securities obscured serious shortages at the end of the five-year period 1981–1985, with 28 percent of the investments still in progress; between 1975 and 1984 hundreds of projects remained unfinished, growth in productivity decreased in relation to the introduction of basic funds, excessive payments were made to labor, and a decline was experienced in housing construction and in various social services, among other ills.

Nevertheless, the revolution continued its socialist plan for the redistribution of social wealth, education, and mass participation. Education recorded revolutionary gains in the 1970s, the health care system took form, Poder Popular was founded and developed, and during the thirteen years of fighting in Angola significant advances were made in internationalism and national political awareness. Gains were made in various areas of the economy, the Party established itself throughout Cuba and made great advances in its internal affairs, other mass organizations were developed, and so forth. The results are contradictory and heterogeneous.

The process of rectification was initiated by Fidel Castro, and he has been the principal force behind it. The question of leadership emerges clearly here. Fidel has fulfilled fundamental roles at every phase of the revolution. The great majority credit him for his role in its inception, the history of the process, present-day society, and, above all, the goals and the plans to which it aspires. People see in him the dialectic of their own power and the power of the revolution that is fundamental to their political life. As trustee of the spiritual unity of the country, naturally it would be Fidel who would denounce contradictions, criticize past mistakes the most harshly, give direction to the rectifying course, and ensure the fraternal relations of all who support the revolutionary cause.[1]

The rectification shuns providential or personalized solutions, recognizing that they are ephemeral and misleading and therefore that the process will be a prolonged one. The problems that have remained unresolved must now be confronted, and it is understood that it would be a mistake to resort to violence, bureaucratic methods, or extremist acts that would compromise the success, the moral strength, and the stability of the process. Mass action is recognized to be based on thoughtful and informed participation, the fundamental strength of popular socialist power.

The rectification addresses the values created by the revolution that shape personal, social, and national expectations. Political unity and anti-imperialist patriotism are strengthened and become more meaningful when they are intimately linked to the concepts of socialism and communism, which are more consistent with the material and spiritual successes of the revolution than with mercantilism, inequality, and the careless enjoyment of the privileges of a life apart from the problems of the people.

Despite the many adverse events of 1989, tributes to those who died in internationalist missions, massive youth demonstrations, and other events celebrated in December of that year and January of 1990 confirmed the support for Cuban socialism of the majority of the people. The national commotion caused by the complicity of certain high military officials with drug trafficking (which does not exist in Cuba) and the corruption of two ministers and other officials had a favorable outcome because all the information was made public by the government and the popular response was one of support for the revolutionary course and for the intensification of rectification.

The great crisis of European socialism in the second half of 1989 did not shake political loyalties on the island, despite the obvious threat to the economy and to national security and the long-standing support for "real" European socialism. Other aspects of revolutionary culture turned out to be more important and decisive. The aggressiveness and intolerance of the United States toward Cuba and throughout the region, attributable to the emergence of a unipolar world order as a consequence of a weakening of the Soviet Union's role as a counterbalance, are not provoking demoralization in Cuba. Quite the contrary; anti-imperialist sentiment and national unity appear stronger, as does support for the government and the Party.

A new generation is now in the majority: 55 percent of the population was born after January 1, 1959, the date of the creation of the new regime. For the past fifteen years education for children through the sixth grade has been universal, and in 1987–1988 35 percent of students were attending primary schools, 55 percent vocational and secondary schools, and 10 percent universities (CEE, 1988:58, 532). Between 1978 and 1986, the educational level of the workers radically improved, which helps explain the successes, the inherent tensions, and, above all, the potential of the Cuban economy.[2]

The youth of Cuba receive a cultural and technical preparation far superior to that of the adult population.[3] However, the dynamic of our economy is inferior to that of our educational system; the technical employment and the utilization of talent are inadequate, and even the general absorption of the young into the work force is limited.[4] There are also contradictions between the type of training received by the young and the specific demands of the work force, between the formal and the real level of graduates, and so forth. The Cuban educational system has failed to transform its curriculum to prepare youth for the realities they will face, which require skills, creativity, and attitudes appropriate to the needs of a small, underdeveloped, Western revolutionary country fighting for socialist development.

The occupational structure of the work force in 1988 reflects the prevailing social order: 94.4 percent work for the state, 4.5 percent are farmers not employed by the state (2.7 percent individual and 1.8 percent participating in cooperatives), 0.8 percent are self-employed, and 0.3 percent are private-salaried workers (CEE, 1988:192). The general tendency has been one of growth for the state, the correction of the resurgence of private production processes and services on a certain scale, and a reduction in the number of private-salaried workers. Criticisms are directed at shortages in products and services, the inferior quality of the latter, poor organization, errors, carelessness, and other flaws in production and distribution. Cuba's primary concerns relate to the diverse and at times contrasting ideas held about rectification—the activity and the perfectibility of socialist society—and not with comparing this society with others that are seeking to privatize enterprises and occupations or increase private initiative.

Successive redistributions of social wealth (including not only social well-being but power), a more broadly defined educational process (for example, the continuum from social coercion to self-education), and the growing participation of the people in education and the direction of social processes are three essential dimensions of this socialist democracy. The rectification consists of separating political activity from deficiencies in the system in order to realize revolutionary socialist progress. The general coherence between mode of production and way of life makes it clear that advances will come from measures promoted within the revolutionary regime and not from forces opposed to it. Once this is clear, we are left only with resolving the difficulties, which are numerous and complex.

We must avoid paying dearly for mistakes that resulted from what were once considered virtues. Decisive as the revolution has been for the process as a whole, it has not produced an effective system of participation, with the result that the tendency has been to wait for guidance from above. Institutionalization brought with it many negative attributes, among them bureaucratism, formalism, and the concealing of deficiencies—all of which have obscured its accomplishments. Yet rather than suggest an institutions versus revolutionary incentive antinomy we wish to create institutions and a system that do not restrain initiative or progress. Unity is indispensable, and it is our strength, but it is not the same thing as unanimity or the suspension of judgment. Diversity enriches society, and that diversity must be promoted and better protected if our revolutionary project is to succeed.

The organized channels through which political and social activity are effectively and systematically accomplished in Cuba form a network that encompasses practically everyone. In addition to the institutions and organizations already mentioned, I would like to emphasize the following: Unión de Jóvenes Comunistas, a selective political organization similar to the Party and guided by it but with very real and specific programs and its own distinctive style; the trade union movement, which has a long and distinguished history and unites nearly all workers in the Central de Trabajadores de Cuba; the Comités de Defensa de la Revolución, the most extensive community organization and one with a vast presence and responsibilities; the Asociación Nacional de Agricultores Pequeños, a revolutionary organization that represents the nonstate sector; the Federación de Mujeres Cubanas, which supports education and the struggle for women's rights with an emphasis on feminine participation; the Federación Estudiantil Universitaria and the Federación Estudiantil de la Enseñanza Media, which, along with the Pioneros (Pioneers), represent children and student youth throughout the country;[5] the militias, comprising almost 2 million men and women, armed and trained; and revolutionary armed forces and their reserves.

These organizations function in accordance with their general guidelines and according to their particular situations; they share the need to participate more effectively in the process of socialist reinforcement. Moreover, the people and the leadership maintain direct communication— one of the basic, enduring features of Fidel's leadership—and this has given rise to organized movements that strongly influence society. An example is the case of the microbrigades, which voluntarily constructed housing and public projects with state support. Although they were eliminated because of the ideas prevailing in the 1970s, they have been revived during the rectification process.

The potential gravity of the economic situation and the difficulties of the conjuncture have influenced the priorities of the rectification process. With various industrial branches only half completed, the looming threat of economic stagnation due to external causes during 1989, the worsening financial situation, the uncertain relations with the Eastern European countries lacking stable food supplies, and so forth, the principal objective has been to survive and guarantee a course of economic development. The criticisms leveled at both the direction and the ideology of the economy in the course of the rectification have been, nevertheless, the premise that was necessary to rally everyone to the task of designing an appropriate and independent strategy for bringing the country prosperity.[6]

It would be misleading, however, to view the economic difficulties as a constant that dominates and constrains policy. Although distorted and bureaucratized socialism fosters lack of interest in the real outcomes of economic processes, saps the enthusiasm that empowers human activity, and sabotages the best-laid plans, the true power of socialism—that of an aware and organized people—can be enhanced by deepening the social revolution in all its aspects. Thus it becomes possible to achieve a genuine ideological understanding of socialist goals for the economy and a systematic and effective political mobilization true to this understanding.

Socialism has to command the economy; without it, the economic tasks of the rectification would be impossible. The problems of participation in the economy, the political process, and the ideal reproduction of the system have proven to be central. There is a need for information and for mechanisms and opportunities for genuine participation in the search for solutions. Clearly this involves a long and difficult process that should not be postponed. There is always immense tension between guaranteeing the continuity of the existing order and promoting the changes in struc- tures and relations that will modify activity in society in the direction of the elimination of all forms of domination.

The agreements reached by the Party's central committee on February 16, 1990, support the rectification process: "Conditions have matured for undertaking in practical and concrete terms the improvement of the political and institutional system of the country"; therefore, "the imme- diate and long-term tasks of the revolution in terms of the management of the Party, the state, the communist youth, the mass organizations, and other institutions, structures and methods" linked to socialist construction will be implemented (*Granma*, February 17, 1990). The agreements were put forth to implement the "turning point" reached the previous summer (see *Granma*, September 2, 1989).[7] It was announced that labor groups would carry out studies and propose measures for improving the structure, contents, methods, and style of the Party's work, beginning with the apparatus of the central committee, in order to increase the operational efficiency of Poder Popular and the work of the mass organizations, "all of which is conceived in direct consultation and with the active participation of the people." A need was recognized to eradicate formalism, bureaucratism, and the emulation of foreign experiments harmful to the internal operations of the Party, the objective being to make it more capable of fulfilling "its two great missions": guiding economic construction and social development and directing and orienting political and ideological work.

According to the text of the agreements, the executive committee of the Council of Ministers, the principal governmental body, which had given top priority to production and services, would have to attend to the institutions not concerned with material production and complete the structure and the national administrative system. The National Assembly was to become a forum in which "the initiatives of the government will find resonance and balance . . . from the perspective of the delegates."[8] In assessing the work of the mass organizations, emphasis was placed on strengthening the labor unions and changes in work methods; direction was also given to the CDRs and the FMC.

The political process just described is valued as a contribution to both the strengthening of the defense of Cuban socialism "faced with the crisis of socialism and the aggressive euphoria of North American imperialism" and the strengthening of the nation and the independence of Cuba; and because it is the progress and not just the longevity of the Cuban Revolution that is at issue, socialism, the sovereignty of Latin America, and the hopes of the Third World are all supported when the revolutionary political process is strengthened.

I have commented on and quoted from this Party document not only because it specifically addresses numerous fundamental questions but because I think that the social conditions exist to make its proposals feasible. Thus, in Cuba, the needs and aspirations of the various elements of society coincide to a far greater degree than the tensions and contradictions. The Cuban system of social relations does not distribute material and spiritual wealth in unequal and exclusionary ways; in fact, it does just the opposite. The challenges to this system today come predominantly not from internal factors but from external ones. The society recognizes the essence of the problems and reinforces unity among its constituent elements. With respect to the deficiencies of the existing regime, the debates and the preoccupations with it reflect a need not to replace the regime but to improve it by deepening its ideals and its socialist project. What is wanted, for example, is not that the state surrender its functions to civil society but rather that it become more efficient and stress its role as an instrument of the revolution while civil society grows stronger and finds deeper meaning for its institutions. The object is to continue to create among the people the fabric that will weave together authority and labor, politics and the economy, civilization and liberation, everyday life and revolutionary tasks, public and private ethics, commitment and leadership, education and the creation of a new culture, motivation, reward, duty, and pleasure.

External circumstances have always played an extraordinary role in Cuban affairs. It is unclear whether the tensions that are developing between specific interests and the homogenizing tendencies that are gaining ground in the world today will grow to critical proportions or remain within manageable bounds. Confronted with these possibilities, Cuba must adhere to its principles and its capacity to defend them while demonstrating flexibility and confidence. In any event, it is clear that its internal situation is decisive for shaping the course of the social process.

Notes

1. Through his vast moral authority, Fidel inspires confidence in lasting revolutionary principles, provides experienced leadership, represents cohesion and unity, provides clarification, and denounces human failings and the shortcomings of the system.

2. The population of Cuba on December 31, 1988, was 10,468,700. The annual rate of growth in this five-year period is estimated at 1 percent. The educational level attained by all workers in 1978 was 54 percent primary, 26 percent secondary, and 3.9 percent university; in 1986 it was 23.5, 37.8, and 9 percent, respectively (CEE, 1987a:203).

3. The 1981 census recorded 2,032,653 people aged seventeen and over, 64 percent of them over forty-five years of age, who had not completed their primary education (CEE, 1987a:540).

4. During 1988 the increase in the number of workers in the state civil sector tripled that recorded in 1987, and 95 percent were in the productive sphere. The rise in employment, though a very positive social measure, negatively affected labor productivity (CEE, 1988:192, 194).

5. The UJC has more than six hundred thousand members, approximately 20 percent of the group from age sixteen to thirty; its fifth congress (April 1987) was a very important occasion for the rectification. The CTC has chapters in all the

labor centers and more than 3 million affiliates; the CDRs have 6.5 million members; the ANAP unites producers who averaged 20.8 percent of the agricultural production in 1981–1988 at constant 1981 prices; the FMC has 3.1 million members.

6. Elements of that strategy involve continuing to develop programs for the production of food, essential for national security and in view of the uncertainty of the external sector, continuing the hydroelectric program, cultivating more crops with irrigation, obtaining more yield per area sown, increasing petroleum production, and continuing the successful development of pharmaceutical production, medical equipment, and the development of biotechnology in general (see Limonta and Padrón in this volume).

7. The editorial asserts that "there exists in what happened a summary of failures that embraces, in one form or another, all the institutions of the Revolution. . . . The improvement of society involves also the improvement of the Party, and this is not only the subject but also the object of the rectification."

8. Fidel explained in a speech before the National Assembly on February 20, 1990, that it was not a matter of organizing the parliament: "Here we will not reproduce the famous division of powers. . . . Here there is one power, the power of the people and the power of the revolution. . . . There is a unity within the state, there are independent functions. . . . The purpose of our rectification is, among other things, to strengthen the revolution, to deepen the revolution" (*Granma*, February 21, 1990).

References

Banco Nacional de Cuba. 1989. *Informe económico* (May). Havana.

Brundenius, Claes. 1985. "Cuba: redistribution and growth with equity," in Sandor Halebsky and John M. Kirk (eds.), *Cuba: Twenty-five Years of Revolution, 1959–1984*. New York: Praeger.

Castro, Fidel. 1990. "Información al pueblo del Comité del Consejo de Ministros." *Granma*, January 22.

CEE (Comité Estatal de Estadísticas). 1987a. *Anuario Estadístico de Cuba*. Havana.

————. 1987b. *Comercio Cuba-Europa Oriental excluida URSS*. Havana.

————. 1987c. *Comercio Cuba-URSS*. Havana.

————. 1988. *Anuario Estadístico de Cuba*. Havana.

————. various years. *Anuario Estadístico de Cuba*. Havana.

Kamorin, A. 1989. "Exportación tropicalizado, o Por qué los *partners* soviéticos y cubanos dejar de entenderse." *Izvestia*, March 8.

Moreno Fraginales, Manuel. 1978. *El ingenio*. Vol. 3. Havana: Ciencias Sociales.

Rodríguez, José Luis. 1986. "Las relaciones económicas Cuba-URSS, 1960–1985." *Temas de Economía Mundial* (17):7–33.

————. 1988. "La erradicación de la pobreza en América Latina: un análisis comparativo de Cuba en el contexto de la región (1959–1986)." *Temas de Economía Mundial* (21).

———— . n.d. "El desarrollo económico de Cuba: resultados y perspectivas." Mimeo. Havana.

Zimbalist, Andrew, and Claes Brundenius. 1989. "Crecimiento con equidad: el desarrollo cubano en una perspectiva comparada." *Cuadernos de Nuestra América* 6 (July-December).

6

Reflections on
the Lessons of Che

Armando Hart Dávalos

Translated by Aníbal Yáñez

Every truly revolutionary moment entails a need to examine its origins. There can be no social or ideological change without reflection upon the past, and not only the recent past but more distant periods. Several examples illustrate this proposition. The ideological, political, and moral transformations that followed the attack on the Moncada barracks in 1953 expressed at once a complete rejection of the immediate past—that is, of the pseudorepublic—and a passionate interest in reclaiming the ideas of José Martí. As the Soviet leadership began to propose renovations that it called revolutionary, one noted an interest in a modern reading of Lenin's works, especially those of his last years. Even renovation movements within Catholicism such as the liberation theology that has arisen in Latin America are marked by an interest in Christianity as it was before the institutionalization of the church—in essence, before the fourth century— and in the effects of its Romanization and Hellenization. If we recall that Hellenization injected into Christianity some of the fundamentals of Greek idealist philosophy, we can appreciate the magnitude of the theoretical problem faced by the liberation theologians. The historical and cultural changes of the European Renaissance also meant both a rejection of the concepts of the immediately preceding centuries and a return to the principles and values of classical Mediterranean antiquity.

In short, when a society is dissatisfied with important aspects of its present and faces problems that arise from its immediate past, it feels the need to reconstruct its history to determine when and how it lost its way.

Although this may foster a certain nostalgia or idealization of the past (this has lately been discussed in the cultural area), from the revolutionary point of view it is something much more constructive. To find new paths and to reach radically different goals tomorrow and the day after, it is necessary to know what happened the day before yesterday. When something of the present is rejected, what is being expressed is the need to affirm something left by the wayside—not to reproduce it exactly (for this would be nostalgic and therefore conservative) but to renew it and make it current with a view to opening the way to a much richer and more promising future.

It has been said that culture is the historical memory of society. In this sense, the rectification that Fidel has called upon us to carry out entails learning what we have forgotten, where we have deviated from our path, and what the younger generations do not know well enough in order to advance more rapidly and firmly. In our revolution there has been no essential or irreparable loss of memory. The past is still present in the minds of many as a reminder to seek new options and new paths. This is precisely what constitutes our revolution's capacity for renovation, and it is sufficiently strong and rich in ideas to deal with errors, deviations, or wrong turns and then take the right path. It is a matter of seeing even our own past from a profoundly revolutionary, innovative perspective, without schemas or stereotypes. Examining the past thirty years of Cuban history from a revolutionary point of view will produce interesting proposals in the most diverse fields. By reviewing the goals that we set for ourselves and the reasons for them we can gather the ideas and stimulus needed to face the future. This is not a matter of emulating the experiences of others; we must reject copying even what we did ourselves, even when we did things right. Rather, it is a matter of studying and reflecting upon the thread that has brought us to the present—a thread with knots created by human stupidity or incompetence or the requirements of the moment.

After listening to the insistent concern expressed at a recent meeting that we were forgetting or even ignoring the significance of our past, a comrade said with some anguish, "It's that we have also forgotten Che." In remembering Che, however, we cannot simply point to his enormous virtues; we need to discover what they represent for the ideas of our revolution. Analysis of the political-ideological range of Che's thought will reveal, among other things, his deep identification with Fidel and with the crucial and decisive problems of our socialist society. It will become clear that he was an opponent of dogmatism and liberal and dissociating tendencies of all kinds. It will also become clear that we need not look far for the paths of the future, the lessons being contained in our own history. The essence of socialism is internationalism, and Cuban cultural history shows an inescapable international vocation.

Four main aspects of Che's life and thought can serve as a framework for our analysis: Che as part of our political and revolutionary history, as a Cuban; Che as a precursor of the new history of the Americas, as a Latin American; Che as a symbol of the Third World; and Che as a communist who denounced the evils and problems besetting socialist societies, as a Marxist-Leninist of the second half of the twentieth century. What I am proposing is not a biography but an examination of the main issues that he confronted. Since this examination must be rigorous and profound, I want to identify some essential features of Che's personality in an effort to move it forward.

One important clue to the essence of Che and to the reason for his currency is that he displayed characteristics often presented as contradictory. He was a synthesis of the man of action and the man of ideas, one who influenced Latin American history and at the same time gave socialism new vigor and richness. The guerrilla, the leader of industry and of the economy, the man of state and of politics was at the same time a tireless researcher, a promoter of new ideas, a fighter of deep intellectual vocation. Explaining his influence may require understanding how he could personify these diverse human virtues. He said of himself that he was an adventurer—the kind that risks his skin to demonstrate the validity of his ideas. Nevertheless, it cannot be said that he was simply a Quixote, his shield on his arm. To do so would be to overlook both essential elements of his life and action and the heroic sense, the vocation of sacrifice, that is present in the consciousness, the culture, and the soul of our America. Che endures not only because he was a brilliant man of action but because his action went hand in hand with a tireless search for correct ideas, for freedom and justice, for social equality among human beings. This is why he is so much among us and daily becomes more so.

The bankruptcy of individualism as a philosophy for egoism is that it insufficiently appreciates the practical consequences of the fact that human beings have social natures that differentiate them from others and it is these that distinguish them from animals. In the social content of their behavior they confirm their singularity and, therefore, their freedom. The problem is that social consciousness cannot simply be imposed in an authoritarian way. Religions from primitive times to the present have postulated that human beings find their fulfillment in dedication to a cause that transcends them and even the materiality of the world. Because of ignorance and group interests, an explanation was sought for individuals' interest in pursuing their social nature that went beyond material reality, and one was found in aspiration to a metaphysical commitment. But individuals' awakening to social consciousness can and must arise from an understanding of their own human condition as social beings— an understanding that confers on them both freedom and a discipline and commitment that not only enrich the spirit but also endow it with immense dignity.

It was this that Che accomplished. One of his fundamental values was self-education and, therefore, self-discipline; he was extremely severe with himself, and this severity was related to the stress that he placed on the individual as a social being. One of the shortcomings of socialist practice is precisely the underestimation of individuality in the educational and political process. Education as a process of individual formation must set itself the task, essentially, of stimulating individuals to exercise self-control and develop their own characters. Educators should aspire to stimulate in individuals a recognition of their own particular virtues, the overcoming of their own defects or limitations, and the development of their own social consciousness.

Social and historical commitment was Che's outstanding virtue, and he took it to heart to enrich his personality, broaden his individual potential, and shape his character as an artist might. He found deep satisfaction in the correspondence between his individual character and commitment to the revolutionary cause. It is this correspondence, through self-education, between the individual and the social that is the core of genuine greatness. Combined with superior intelligence and an indomitable will, it made it possible for him to reach the highest form of humanity: the revolutionary. Perhaps his most important lesson for those who would attempt to follow his example is that the higher individual, the true human being as a social being, can find genuine happiness in commitment to the revolutionary cause. This commitment is not metaphysical, nor does it transcend the materiality of the world; it is at the very root of humankind's social vocation.

There is another, more profound and universal meaning to Che's life that merits special reflection in these times. He must be considered one of the great prognosticators of the need for revolutionary changes in socialism. From the beginning of the 1960s, he understood problems as no one else did at the time, and, whatever one's conclusions with regard to the value of some of his concrete proposals, the analysis of these problems has unquestionable historical validity. What is more, life has proven him fundamentally right. In essence, the current process of rectification of errors in our society has to do with problems that Che pointed out. His fundamental concern in this regard had to do with the role of ideology—of moral development, of education in the paths of socialism. He was a sworn enemy of administrative red tape, and he also understood the negative influence of a commodity spirit (herein lies one of the elements of the deep identity of thought between Fidel and Che that I have referred to), two great problems that strongly affected the processes of socialism then and later.

Today there is much talk of the importance of analyzing the ideological, theoretical, and political debates of the 1920s in the Soviet Union. Antecedents are being sought for some of the important problems of the period following the establishment of the New Economic Policy and especially following Lenin's dramatic death. From the early years after the triumph of the Cuban Revolution, however, Che insisted that this was the indispensable starting point for discussion, and in this he was a visionary.

An essential aspect of the Leninist position with regard to economic policy in the Soviet Union in the 1920s was the utilization of an "original state capitalism," but in the hands of the working class, as a possible line of retrenchment. Che recognized that, whereas in Lenin's time the methods of economic management inherited from capitalism were part of the framework of competitive capitalism, in the Cuba of the 1960s what was inherited in decisive sectors of the economy were methods characteristic of monopoly capitalism, including finance and other technical-economic features as important principles of economic management. His essential contribution in this field is to have proposed the use of finance in economic management by the socialist state. In other words, rather than disdaining economic principles and relying solely upon ideological-cultural ones, he advocated methods of management and control backed by historical practice in capitalist societies (although of course on a radically different plane) as technological instruments for achieving socialist objectives. The discovery of economic-social methods of conscious management to counteract the spontaneous action of contradictory particular interests is an intellectual feat that should inspire the deepest reflection. This is one line of thought that researchers might well consider in examining the currency of Che's ideas.

Of course, this is not to say that one should limit oneself to study of the formulas Che advanced. Rather, as Fidel has said, it is impossible to reach any conclusion—especially given our country's circumstances—without taking his ideas about the processes of economic and social construction into account. Nobody is proposing mechanical copying, nor would Che himself have allowed it. What is being suggested is that his ideas be taken as a guide for an analysis of the evolution of Cuban economic and political thought. Without understanding the essence of the issues he raised a quarter of a century ago, it will be impossible to find practical, concrete, and immediate solutions to our most serious problems.

Che was never dogmatic. He was a deadly enemy of petrified formulas, a staunch partisan of the search for truth and the analysis of problems in the spirit of creativity. But he was also a model of intellectual and revolutionary discipline and an advocate of individual responsibility. Thus, his personality sums up the struggle against dogmatism and against liberalism—a difficult task, but then he was never one to take the easy road. Beyond this, he demonstrated that in a genuine revolutionary intellectual rigor is not theoreticism or academicism, much less an intellectualism detached from real life or a hypercritical spirit incapable of understanding how things are transformed—all expressions of intellectual mediocrity. He demanded that thought, intelligence, and creativity be open, and he fought vigorously against liberalism and indiscipline. Thus, he could be a model for the revolutionary intellectual of our time.

In recognition of our people and consideration of Che's internationalist spirit, it must be said that his merit is also in great measure theirs. The narrow nationalism that has prevented some from contributing to a great history has never spread among us. From the moment Che joined Fidel's struggle, we all saw the presence of an Argentine in our war as a natural thing. An internationalist temperament is deeply rooted in Cuban culture. It is not easy to find historical examples of this spirit, and therefore the fact that he was welcomed here and exalted as an outstanding son— placed on the highest pedestal of history—reflects very favorably not only on him but also on the Cuban people.

In the history of the Cuban Revolution, the modern history of Latin America, and the history of socialism, Che's essence and his ideas—along with his creative spirit, his discipline, his Latin Americanism, his internationalism, his deep love of humanity, his communist passion, and his determination to confront imperialism in the Americas or anywhere else on earth—form a link without which it will be impossible to face the future. In one way or another, decisive battles against imperialism will take place, and socialism will triumph; then Che will take on the enormous dimensions of a forerunner of the new America.

The symbol of Che that has spread around the world stands for a vocation of service to humanity in action and thought. It represents an epoch that will endure because it contains an idea of human redemption that on this continent has acquired universal dimensions. New times will see changes of the most diverse kind. Although the paths of these changes will be many, on all of them will be borne the memory of that genuinely American man who arrived in Mexico from Buenos Aires having passed through Arbenz's Guatemala, who met Fidel, who came on the *Granma*, who became one of the most important leaders in Cuba's history, and who later, with a firm internationalist—especially Latin Americanist— vocation, traveled thousands of kilometers to defend freedom all over the world.

PART 2
Economic Development

7

The Creativity of
Che's Economic Thought

Carlos Tablada

Translated by Michael Baumann

As part of the rectification process, Fidel has proposed a thorough study of Ernesto Che Guevara's writings on the building of socialism and communism. Che's thought constitutes a rich source of ideas and solutions—socialist formulas for constructing the new society. Every socialist country faces the dual problem of establishing an efficient system of economic administration and management and creating new human values free of individualism and selfishness. Thus the communist education of working people is an essential part of creating and extending socialist society. The international context has changed in the last twenty years, but in terms of the concrete historical, social, and economic problems faced by Asia, Africa, Latin America, and even the developed countries the situation is essentially the same as the one Che confronted. If there is any real difference, it is that the contradictions and conflicts have deepened. Poverty, exploitation, homelessness, and inequality have increased; the foreign debt has risen a hundredfold; the world we live in has become more explosive.

Some people in Cuba today recognize only Che's contribution in the application of Marxism-Leninism, and they often contend that the budgetary finance system he created was suited solely to the concrete needs

This chapter reprinted by permission of Pathfinder Press. A different and longer version appears in English translation in issue no. 8 of the magazine *New International*.

of the first stage of the revolution. Accepting these two premises tends to make it impossible to use more than a few isolated ideas far from the center of his thought: his rigorous standards, his emphasis on financial controls (accounting, cost analysis, auditing), and the priority he gave to organization. To grasp the value of Che's thought for the building of socialism and communism, we must examine his theoretical and practical contributions more deeply. As Fidel has pointed out, explaining and systematizing Che's contribution to the theory and practice of Marxism-Leninism is the fundamental starting point for fully resolving our problems.

Twenty-five years ago Che, along with Fidel, recognized the stagnation, schematism, and dogmatism of an important current of revolutionary thought. Che and Fidel had the same principles, fought for the same objectives, and shared a belief in the possibility of transforming human beings. In 1979, Fidel summed up their common view of economic development as follows: "Development primarily involves attention to human beings, who should be the protagonists and the goal of all development efforts" (Castro, 1981:204). Che did not view economic development as an end in itself. For him development had meaning only if it served to transform men and women, enhance their creative capacities, and draw them beyond self-centeredness. The transition to the kingdom of freedom was a voyage from "me" to "us," and socialism could not accomplish this transition with what he called "the dull instruments left to us by capitalism" (Guevara, 1987:250). It was impossible to advance toward communism if life under socialism was organized, as in the previous society, like competition among wolves.

It is obvious that it would make no sense to try to apply mechanically every formula or solution that Che proposed and put into practice more than twenty years ago. Che himself would not have done so; it was not his way of thinking. Cuban society and the international context have changed during the intervening period. I suspect, however, that the system of managing the economy that arises out of the rectification process—whatever name it is given—will stem not from the economic accounting system but from the thought of Che and Fidel. Any evaluation we make should be based on a full, unprejudiced, and objective assessment of the experience of building socialism in Cuba over the last thirty years, on an assessment of the experiences of building socialism in other parts of the world, and on communist ideals and Marxist-Leninist theory.

Applying Che's Ideas Today

The fundamental aspects of Che's ideas and practice remain, in my opinion, applicable today. Adjustments must be made to take account of changes that have occurred since then, but this must be done *without altering his fundamental starting point*—his critical approach to certain conceptions of the way to build socialism during the transition to communist society.

Beginning from an understanding that "communism is a phenomenon of consciousness and not solely a phenomenon of production" (Guevara, 1966:423), Che devoted himself to the task of creating a system of economic management that, while maintaining this focus, would draw upon advanced accounting techniques that permitted more effective controls and an efficient centralized management; studies and practical application of the methods of centralization and decentralization used by the capitalist monopolies; the application of mathematical methods and computer techniques to the economy; techniques of programming and supervising production; budgetary techniques as instruments of planning and supervision through finance; administrative techniques of implementing economic controls; participation by the masses in the management of the economy, direct motivation of the worker, and workers' identification with the final product; and the practical and theoretical experiences of the socialist countries.

For Che, the building of socialism and communism was not simply an administrative, technical, and economic task but also one demanding an ideological and political approach. He stressed the integration of all these elements in a conception of the economic management system needed to build socialism, the budgetary finance system. He insisted that the fundamental element was the development of consciousness, the ultimate objective being a new human being. Simultaneously with creating the new material and technical foundations for socialism it was necessary to establish a system of education that ensured the development of consciousness and, consequently, the formation of new men and women. With the budgetary finance system, he sought to organize the economy and attain maximum efficiency in economic management, to deepen and develop the consciousness of the masses, and to unify and develop the world socialist system. He called on the Party and the youth organization to serve as the agents of an extensive attempt at political education.

Few people are aware that the budgetary finance system worked very efficiently during the opening years of the revolution despite the circumstances then prevailing nationally and in the Ministry of Industry. At the time, the ministry directed 70 percent of the country's industrial production (sugar, light industry, basic industry, a sector of the food industry, machine tools, construction materials, pharmaceuticals, and others). It had responsibility for some 260,000 workers, forty-eight consolidated enterprises, and about fifteen hundred establishments. In all, it administered basic means of production valued at 1.5 billion pesos, of which

930 million were of capitalist origin (Tablada, 1989). Enormous obstacles were presented by the U.S. blockade, the loss of experts and trained administrative personnel through emigration to the United States, a shortage of technicians and trained personnel of all types (for example, the Ministry of Industry and all its departments never had more than 473 engineers at one time),[1] difficulties caused by shortages of spare parts, raw materials, and equipment, a million people only recently literate, a work force with low levels of skill, lack of discipline among workers, and reliance on administrators who often had no more than a second-grade education. Do Cuban enterprises today match the level of organization, controls, management, efficiency, and systematization that had been reached by the enterprises consolidated under Che in December 1964? From my personal experience, I believe the answer is no. We have not matched them in terms of financial discipline in billing and payment, inventory control, accuracy and truthfulness in primary data, or cost analysis at the level of the production unit.

It has been suggested that we adopt some of the subsystems that made up the budgetary finance system, grafting them onto the economic accounting system. But the budgetary finance system is a coherent whole; it has an internal structure based on theoretical and practical premises that have been fully substantiated. Indeed, its character as a *system* is one of its most vital features. Che developed it because he did not accept the economic accounting system. It *has no antecedents* and is not to be confused, simply because of its name, with budgetary systems used earlier in sister socialist countries and later in our country. In its fundamental principles and methods, the budgetary finance system is unique.

Economic Planning and Political Consciousness

The relationship between Che's general conception of the political economy of socialism, his theoretical views on the period of the transition to socialism, and his views on the different systems of economic management has been subjected to the most varied interpretations. Some say that there is no such relationship, and others say that if one exists it is not essential. This reflects a failure to grasp the creativity and scope of Che's outstanding contribution.

As I have pointed out elsewhere (1989), it is important to differentiate between the technical and the political aspects of managing the economy. Che argued that technical procedures could be taken from wherever they were the most developed. The new society could adapt them to its needs without fear of contagion by bourgeois ideology, *so long as the process was limited* to the adoption or assimilation of technical norms of managing and instituting controls over production. From the point of view of ideology, however, he held that the new society should not rely on economic mechanisms, incentives, and management criteria that pertained to the capitalist mode of production. In other words, he called for critical assimilation of the most advanced techniques in economic management and control over production, but with regard to motivating the producers he rejected the dull instruments left to us by capitalism. The transition to socialism and communism need not, even in its first moments, have its character determined by the law of value and the other market-economy categories that it implies; the operation of the law of value should be approached as simply one of the limitations we have inherited from capitalism.

Che believed that political economy in the Soviet Union and the Eastern European countries had not fully grasped and developed what was new in socialist and communist society. He called for giving more thought to the fundamental laws of economics, stressing the moral and political factor. He felt that economic planning should be viewed as humanity's first chance to harness economic forces. Developing the thought of Marx, Engels, and Lenin, he linked economic planning to the concepts of the anticapitalist revolution and the dictatorship of the proletariat. In this context, economic planning marks the emergence of a new way of making history. For the first time in history, humanity has taken on the role of consciously transforming society.

Economic planning is the only instrument that makes it possible to develop the productive forces, form new human relations, create the new human being, and achieve the stage of communist society. It is not, however, a panacea. The economic plan is created by human beings and is part of a general conception. Neither a fetish nor a straitjacket, it is a basic tool for building socialist society. Thus to reduce the concept of planning to its economic components would be to distort it from the outset and limit its possibilities. In Che's opinion, the plan embraced *material relations as a whole* (in Marx's sense) and therefore should combine creating the foundation for the economic development of the new society, as well as for economic regulation and controls, and creating a new type of human relations and a new human being.

A principle of the transition to communism that cannot be overlooked without distorting the plan and endangering that transition is that the effectiveness of the plan cannot be evaluated *solely* in terms of whether or not it improves economic management and therefore augments the goods available to society or in terms of the income obtained in the production process. The real measure of its effectiveness lies in its potential for improving economic management in the direction of the central objective, communist society. In other words, the true gauge is the plan's ability to combine what is rational economically with what is rational socially—the degree to which the economic apparatus helps create the technical and material base for the new society and *at the same time* spurs a transformation in the habits and values of those who participate in the productive process, thereby helping to create and instill the new communist values.

Methods Borrowed from Capitalism

Because of the way it functions, the economic accounting system is inseparably linked to the dull instruments left to us by capitalism. It cannot work without capitalist economic mechanisms and categories borrowed from the capitalist market system, and it assimilates these mechanisms and categories not as limitations but as virtues. Using these categories and the economic and social structures and relations they describe in capitalist society makes it difficult, however, to deal with a reality whose characteristics are not theoretically understood. The law of value is an element of Marxist economic theory that has been torn out of its context as the fundamental law of motion of capitalism and converted into a fundamental pillar of more than one theory on the political economy of the transition to socialism. Che's critical analysis of such use of the law of value is one of his greatest contributions to Marxist-Leninist theory.

His position can be summed up as follows: Rejecting the law of value as the guiding principle in the transition to communism, he distinguished between acknowledging the existence of a series of capitalist relations that necessarily persist during the transition (including the law of value, given its character as an economic law—that is, as an expression of certain economic tendencies) and suggesting the possibility of managing the economy by the conscious and fundamental use of the law of value and its corollaries. He denied that the transition to communism—even in its first phases—had to unfold in accordance with the law of value and the other categories of commodity production implied by its use and that the monetary-commodity relations that reached their highest development under capitalism had to be developed in the transition period as a vehicle for achieving communist society. He rejected the idea that it was impossible to avoid using "the *commodity* category in relations among state enterprises," considering "all such establishments to be part of the single large enterprise that is the state" (Guevara, 1987:220). He held it necessary to implement economic policies that would lead to the gradual withering away of the old relations, including the market, money (so long as its functions were distorted), and thus the lever of direct material self-interest, or, better, would lead to the elimination of the conditions that gave rise to these relations:

We understand that capitalist categories are retained for a time and that the length of this time cannot be determined beforehand. But the characteristics of the transition period are those of a society throwing off its old bonds in order to arrive quickly at the new stage.

The *tendency* must be, in our opinion, to eliminate as vigorously as possible the old categories, including the market, money, and, therefore, the lever of material interest—or, to put it better, to eliminate the conditions for their existence. (Guevara, 1987:219)

He warned against the indiscriminate use of capitalist categories such as the commodity as the economic cell, profitability, and individual material interest as a lever (Guevara, 1987:250) in building the new society, arguing that they would rapidly take on an existence of their own, in the end imposing their own influence on human relations. He explained that giving free rein to the law of value in the transition to communism would make it impossible to restructure social relations fundamentally because it meant perpetuating the "umbilical cord" that tied alienated man to society.

In our view communism is a phenomenon of consciousness and not solely a phenomenon of production. We cannot arrive at communism through the simple mechanical accumulation of quantities of goods made available to the people. By doing that we would get somewhere, to be sure, to some peculiar form of socialism. But what Marx defined as communism, what is aspired to in general as communism, cannot be attained if man is not conscious, that is, if he does not have a new consciousness toward society. (Guevara, 1966:423)

Che's budgetary finance system recognized the law of value, monetary-commodity relations, and the commodity as such, but only in relations between the state, cooperatives, and individuals and in foreign trade. It rejected the use of monetary-commodity relations between state enterprises. The transition required the development of new socialist relations in the course of which the law of value would gradually wither away.

As the means of production were transferred to the revolutionary state, new relations of production would emerge and become established. This stage would require a new conception of production—of its inner workings and its goals—and new ways of operating the mechanisms of supervision, organization, management, and incentives. During this stage some means of production would remain in the hands of capitalists and small producers, both private and cooperative. Even while commodity production still existed for a sector of production, however, measures taken by the revolutionary state on social questions as well as on strictly economic ones would tend to modify the way in which the law of value functioned.

These measures would include, among others, lowering the rent on housing, providing medical care and social assistance either free of charge or at "below-market prices," setting and controlling prices to combat counterrevolutionary speculation, establishing control over foreign currency, foreign trade, and domestic wholesale trade, bringing previously marginalized sectors of the population into the economic life of the country, and taking steps to eliminate unemployment.

In practice, such measures *would make it impossible for the law of value to rule.* It would no longer establish the quantities in which commodities were produced or exchanged. It would no longer determine how labor power was allotted among different sectors of the economy or how resources were allocated. It would cease to be a regulatory mechanism. Of key importance in this regard is that prices would no longer be set spontaneously through the market fluctuations in supply and demand that are responsible for the automatic, anarchic, and brutal way in which proportions and equilibrium are established in capitalist society. In this stage of the revolution the leadership would establish distribution not on the basis of value but in accordance with its political program, the concrete conditions of the country and the rest of the world, and the revolution's political, ideological, and military strength.

What is important in the management of society's productive forces is the analysis of economic and social costs and benefits overall. This means that on the basis of a rigorous analysis of the costs of production and the value of the goods produced, socialism can rationally set prices above or below the value of a particular item. In other words, the prices of particular items become interchangeable so long as required levels of "profitability" (understood as equilibrium in the management of society's productive resources—meaning nothing more than the existence of a surplus product) and efficiency are maintained overall and the sum total of the prices tends to coincide with the value created.

This might be taken as proof that in the final analysis the law of value does govern under socialism—that it regulates the overall economic and social equilibrium—but this is an illusion. Ensuring the necessary social surplus product is a feature inherent in any society if it is to continue to exist, but this elementary principle—this measure of economic rationality—*is not* the law of value. The law of value is simply the theory that explains *the manner* in which this equilibrium is established—spontaneously—in bourgeois society. The plan, for its part, is *the manner* in which this equilibrium is attained—consciously and rationally—in socialist and communist societies.

The advantages of the plan in comparison with capitalism do not, however, rest in its establishing the cost of manufacturing a given product in order to set its price. The plan has a different task: to serve as a tool in rationally and consciously building the new society. Its main advantage is precisely that, unlike the capitalist business executive, it is not bound by the level of profitability of a particular production unit or even an entire sector of production. Everything it manages can be financed centrally and regulated on the basis of overall proportions. The key to its success is the rigor, detail, precision, and accuracy of both the data at its disposal and the analysis of those data. The aim is to establish the proportions that ensure the successful reproduction of the relations of socialist production.

Che saw cost analysis as the fundamental way of measuring the efficiency of establishments and enterprises. He pointed to its usefulness as a method of supervision and management. He viewed it as the ideal way to optimize the expenditure of social labor, making it possible to reduce the amount of such labor per unit produced and thereby increase—in real terms—the productivity and efficiency of establishments, enterprises, branches of industry, and society as a whole.

The foregoing is essential for understanding the new ideas put forward by Che and the Cuban Revolution in this domain. It is not that Che wanted to skip stages and rush things, and he had no illusions that an accelerated development of consciousness could impose a faster pace than history allowed.

We should not forget that today—almost thirty-six years after the attack on the Moncada garrison[2] and thirty years after the triumph of the revolution—there are some who still do not understand the essence of our revolution. It has been, ever since Moncada, a "revolt against oligarchies and against revolutionary dogmas" (Guevara, 1968). Che said that we had to concern ourselves from the beginning with the creation of a new consciousness and a new morality and that this had to occur simultaneously with efforts to develop the material and technical foundations of the new society. He understood that the new consciousness would inevitably emerge from a gradual process of transformation of social structures and that the possibilities for transforming humankind were therefore determined more by the transformation of the social relations of production and the correct selection of the motivating levers than by appeals to consciousness.

"The law of value and the plan are two terms linked by a contradiction and its resolution," he pointed out. "Centralized planning is the mode of existence of socialist society, its defining characteristic, and the point at which man's consciousness finally succeeds in synthesizing and directing the economy toward its goal: the full liberation of the human being within the framework of communist society" (Guevara, 1987:220).

In a society based on the production of commodities, production, distribution, and the reproduction of congealed social labor are determined *after the fact.* In socialist society, however, these elements can be determined *at the outset* through economic planning. The problem lies in the ideological influence that commodity fetishism continues to exert over the consciousness of the individual. During the transition to socialism, people continue to believe that they are seeing the law of value, commodities, and monetary-commodity relations when in reality they are witnessing their opposites:

> We believe that the inconsistency among the defenders of the economic accounting system stems from the fact that they follow Marxist analysis to a certain point but then, in order to continue their line of argument, they have to take a leap (leaving the "missing link" in the middle). Concretely, the defenders of the economic accounting system have never correctly explained how the concept of the commodity, in its essence, can be applied to transactions [among enterprises and institutions] in the state sector. Nor have they explained how the law of value can be used "intelligently" in the socialist sector, with its distorted markets. (Guevara, 1977:103–104)

Profit vs. Social Needs

The economic accounting system fosters a certain fetishism. The category of profit tends to obscure and divert attention from the essential point, production—producing the variety of goods required to meet social needs. The economic accounting system measures production efficiency by profit and profitability. These are, however, categories that in essence pertain to the market—that attain their fullest development under capitalism—and in the process of developing they tend to impede what is the central aim of socialism, the creation of the use values that are essential to the satisfaction of needs.

Marx explained that in bourgeois capitalist societies based on commodity production, private ownership determines that the only means isolated producers have to relate to one another is through the market. The varying quantities of labor to be expended are thus regulated after the fact, in an anarchic and spontaneous way. Value itself serves as the fundamental criterion in the process of expending labor. In socialist society, however, the means of production are socially owned. Use values, the practical features of commodities, and the quantity and quality of a product become the fundamental elements of exchange. From the outset, economic planning permits regulation of the various activities that the producers should maintain among themselves. For the first time, there is a *direct* relationship between consumer needs and what is produced.

In capitalist society, this relationship is indirect and bears the hallmarks of fetishism. Relations between human beings take on the appearance of relations between things. The real aim of production becomes the commodity's brief moment in the marketplace. The commodity, an inert object, becomes the regulator of activity among human beings. In socialist society, in contrast, there is a direct relationship between human needs and the form in which those needs are satisfied. This relationship is established through planning prior to the initiation of the process of production. The commodity no longer comes first, ahead of the human being. Work is directly social. The producer's main attention is focused on the useful, practical, and tangible aspects of work, on its qualitative and quantitative character (including economizing in the expenditure of social labor). Value appears directly as a social relationship of production, consciously established.

Recent experiences in both Cuba and other countries that use the economic accounting system make one thing clear: There is a definite tendency under this system for the production of use values to become secondary, despite its fundamental importance in the transition to socialism. This exercise in fetishism in turn gives rise to additional monetary-commodity relations. The economic stagnation and exhaustion that accompany the use of the economic accounting system demand—in return for continuing to develop the economy—new and deeper monetary-commodity relations, that is, new steps backward.

Historically, the process of exchange has in practice increasingly departed from the law of value.[3] It is only in less-developed commodity-producing societies that this law operated in its pure form.

In my view, fetishism gains ground in man's consciousness when there is a failure to recognize that, of three elements basic to the existence and development of commodity relations, two have disappeared or tend to disappear or diminish during the transition period. These two elements are private ownership of the means of production (which is fundamental) and relative economic isolation. The latter tends to decline gradually as society becomes more integrated. From the outset social ownership of the means of production gradually imbues work with a directly social character. The tendency is therefore to reduce the social and economic differences among producers, not to deepen them.

We are masters of the means of production and of our destiny, but the fetishism created by the economic accounting system prevents individuals from feeling a part of this process. In fact, far from eliminating alienation, it actually increases it to the extent that it promotes creating and obtaining values (money) as opposed to the use values that alone are capable of satisfying human needs. The fetishism inherent in the economic accounting system stems from the fetishism of monetary-commodity relations. Indeed, it promotes an extension and reinforcement of those relations.

Che sought to combine, in one vital and unified body of theory, economic production and the production and reproduction of the mode of activity in which economic production occurs—that is, to include in his theory the social relations that individuals establish both within and outside the process of production. In other words, he believed that there were concerns above and beyond simply producing more, concerns having to do with what is produced, how, why, for whom, and to what end. We must produce material goods, but at the same time we must produce the person who will run the machinery—who will keep track of, oversee, administer, supervise, and direct the process of production.

Che understood that if people live, work, and act under the effects of capitalist, commodity-based, or pseudocapitalist mechanisms, no amount of political work can transform them into models of the new morality. If the mechanisms compel one to act as a capitalist administrator, a "market fanatic," a "two-bit businessman," or a worker motivated by direct material self-interest through the use of money, one cannot think or act as a worker motivated by the interests of society as a whole. One cannot become a better human being. Social being determines social consciousness. That is why he designed a system—the budgetary finance system—that took existing limitations into account but also promoted a new attitude toward work. He was convinced that consciousness would engender consciousness, virtue and faithfulness would engender virtue and faithfulness, honesty would engender honesty, and a good example would multiply good examples.

Che took up a theme that was incomprehensible to many of his contemporaries and remains so to some people today: the relationship between base and superstructure, between social being and social consciousness under socialism, between the modification of the conditions of life and the modification of human activity, between the production of life and the production of consciousness. Generally speaking, discussion of a crisis in the functioning of a socialist economy usually revolves around economic efficiency, concentrating on the technical and administrative aspects of the problem. The social, political, and ideological dimensions of the alternatives under debate are not taken up. The superstructure, or part of it, is dismissed from consideration; meanwhile the *base* remains free of all suspicion. This error presents a danger. The superstructure can be adversely affected by economic relations, but, as history has shown, if it is left out of a discussion of the possible transformation of economic relations a general retreat in social consciousness may well set in.

Che pointed to this dialectical relationship. He emphasized that market-economy mechanisms tended to impose their own independent dynamic on social relations as a whole. He said that the same thing was true when direct material incentives were indiscriminately and unthinkingly used as the driving force of production. Direct material incentives were for him "the great Trojan horse of socialism," undermining the socialist system from within and leading to backtracking in consciousness and social relations. He called for the identification of structures that give rise to selfishness and personal ambition in order to replace them with new institutions and social mechanisms capable of molding future generations differently. This is not romanticism but Marxist-Leninist understanding that social being determines social consciousness and that the transformation of both can only be resolved in practice and hand in hand.

In short, Che's transitional model was conceived not in order to adapt to this reality but to transform it. His analysis did not end here, however. It went on to describe what would result from following the beaten track of capitalism—in particular its impact on the relationship between social being and social consciousness.

Che and the New Economic Policy

I have elsewhere analyzed Che's ideas on the New Economic Policy (NEP) initiated under Lenin's leadership in the young Soviet republic in 1921 (Tablada, 1989:96–106; Guevara, 1987:206–208). Here I want to stress only that under the NEP the superstructure had an increasingly marked influence on relations of production, and the conflict provoked by the creation of this hybrid tended to resolve itself in favor of the superstructure, leading to new retreats.

On the basis of Marx, Che took up the theory of value, thinking about it creatively under present-day circumstances. He perceived that the political economy of socialism had adopted this theory uncritically and extrapolated from it on the basis of limited experience. It had not stopped to consider the transition in sufficient depth. This was one of the main reasons for the incorrectness, dogmatism, superficial analysis, scholasticism, inconsistent pragmatism, and schematism that characterize what increasingly came to be presented as the political economy of socialism following Lenin's death. As a result of his serious and scientific study of the NEP period, Che presented a totally new and original vision based on the principles and specific elements of Marxist theory.

Che and Fidel share the merit of having pointed out these deficiencies twenty-five years ago. Che in particular indicated their source and characterized the principles and foundations of political economy in the transition to socialism. I have pointed out the harm that has been done and continues to be done by trying to use the dull instruments of capitalism to build socialism. Che foresaw that employing the economic accounting system in any country would undermine the cohesiveness of the socialist camp as a whole. By exacerbating individualism, selfishness, and nationalism, it would seriously endanger internationalist consciousness and its effective practice both among the socialist countries themselves and in their relations with the underdeveloped world.

Through Che's speeches at various international forums, the leadership of the Cuban Revolution raised for the first time the injustice of unequal trade and the foreign debt (Guevara, 1987:299–320, 337–346). Trade between socialist countries cannot be governed by the law of value. The determination of a *just* price must take into consideration the true costs of a developing socialist country's social labor. This is because the real foundation of value is in the expenditure of physical and mental energy by the producer in the process of production—creating value. The problems of productivity and labor intensity are derived from this, and, although important, they can be separated from the process of expending social labor. In the end, this process is the foundation of any creation of value and wealth.

Che as Contemporary

Minimizing the differences between the budgetary finance and economic accounting systems might at first glance seem logical, but a detailed analysis of the contradictions between the two systems leads to a different conclusion: The underlying problems cannot be resolved simply by indiscriminately grafting elements of one system onto the other. It should not be forgotten that the budgetary finance system created by Che "is part of a general conception of the development of building socialism and must therefore be studied in its totality" (Guevara, 1966:387). Che once commented on the capabilities of the budgetary finance system and the economic accounting system in terms of prioritizing material or moral incentives. He noted that the budgetary finance system could move forward with a partial use of material incentives, if so desired, but a combination of "moral incentives with financial self-management is impossible; before it even takes a couple of steps the system will get tangled in its own feet and fall on its face" (Guevara, 1966:447).

Studying Che's thought and action has nothing to do with celebrating one more anniversary; this is not a question of conjuncture. Rather, rectification time is also Che's time. Che is not part of the past; his thought and action are not limited in application solely to the concrete conditions of the early years of the revolution. Nor is Che just for the future; he was not simply the architect of a more perfect system of ideas, a more perfect society, closer to communism. I submit that Che is part of the present, *our present*. If we want the men and women of today to begin to be like Che, if we want our children to become the new men and women of the twenty-first century, we must begin by understanding that Che is first of all a man of the twentieth century and that his ideas were intended for this century—for beginning to create today the human being of tomorrow.

In his remarks on October 8, 1987, Fidel called on our young people, our economists, our students, our cadres in the Party and the state—on our entire people—to study and absorb Che's political and economic thought. He said that this was an absolute necessity for the development of our political education—for combating disorientation and blind imitation of and intoxication with a single type of idea, becoming more alert and more consistent revolutionaries, and finding new solutions to problems both old and new. "I want our people to become a people of ideas, of concepts," Fidel said. "I want them to analyze those ideas, think about them, and, if they want, discuss them" (Tablada, 1989:49).

We should always remember Che's words in his notes on "Socialism and Man in Cuba": "Socialism is young and has its mistakes. We revolutionaries often lack the knowledge and intellectual daring needed to meet the task of developing the new man with methods different from the conventional ones—and the conventional methods suffer from the influences of the society that created them" (Guevara, 1987:256).

Notes

1. The figures in this paragraph come from Miguel Figueras Pérez, who was general director of planning and perspectives in the ministry during the period in which Che headed it.

2. On July 26, 1953, Fidel Castro led an attack on the Moncada army garrison in Santiago de Cuba that marked the beginning of the revolutionary struggle against the regime of Fulgencio Batista. After the attack's failure, Batista's forces massacred more than fifty of the captured revolutionaries. Castro and others were taken prisoner, tried, and sentenced to prison. They were released in May 1955 after a public defense campaign forced the regime to issue an amnesty.

3. *First distortion*—free enterprise capitalism: cost of production (law of value) $C + V + S$, market price $C + V + P'$. *Second distortion*—pure monopoly capitalism: monopoly price = price of production + monopoly factors. *Third distortion*— state monopoly capitalism: monopoly prices along with extensive state intervention + elements of international economic relations, including such factors as transnationalization of capital and production, unequal exchange, price setting by international monopolies, the arms race and the military-industrial complex, the policy of subsidies, and protectionism. *Fourth distortion*—emergence of socialist society, transition. *Total elimination*—communist society.

References

Castro, Fidel. 1981. *Fidel Castro Speeches: Cuba's Internationalist Foreign Policy, 1975–80*. New York: Pathfinder.

Guevara, Ernesto Che. 1966. *El Che en la revolución cubana.* Vol. 6. Havana: Educación Ministerio del Azúcar.

————. 1968. *The Diary of Che Guevara.* New York: Bantam Books.

————. 1977. *Escritos y discursos.* Vol. 8. Havana: Ciencias Sociales.

————. 1987. *Che Guevara and the Cuban Revolution: Writings and Speeches of Ernesto Che Guevara.* New York: Pathfinder.

Tablada, Carlos. 1989. *Che Guevara: Economics and Politics in the Transition to Socialism.* New York: Pathfinder.

8

Cuban Economic Policy in the Process of Rectification

José Luis Rodríguez García

Translated by Philip R. Martínez

Every revolutionary process takes place in the midst of complex conditions that involve both advances and setbacks. These are the practical and inevitable consequences of the search for solutions to the problems created by the construction of socialism. The conscious participation of each individual in this revolutionary task is necessarily linked to a process of development that entails not only economic growth and the advance of basic social services but also the transformation of people as social beings (Guevara, 1977). The methods adopted to ensure the fulfillment of each of these objectives require attention to and precise assessment of numerous factors at each historical moment, and this is not always achieved.

This process has been especially complex in countries such as Cuba that started from a low level of development. Economic policy over the course of the past thirty years has, however, experienced undeniable successes as well as failures despite the significant difficulties normally associated with any development process and the hostility that it has confronted because of its socialist orientation (Zimbalist and Eckstein, 1987; Brundenius, 1984; Mesa-Lago, 1981; Rodríguez, 1984, 1989). Perhaps one of the most important aspects of the Cuban case is the consistently flexible and self-critical position that has permitted errors to be corrected and lessons to be learned. For example, as early as 1963 a critical revision was made in the strategy of accelerated industrialization so as to create more adequate foundations for the industrialization process.

The first half of the 1960s was a period of research and experimentation during which the mechanisms most appropriate for the construction of socialism were utilized. From 1967 to 1970, however, economic policy adopted an idealistic approach that denied monetary and commercial operations any role in socialism. These policies were critically evaluated and corrected between 1971 and 1975 (PCC, 1978:102–111). Taking this into consideration, the present process of rectification can be viewed as part of the historical task of searching for the best ways to construct socialism in Cuba.

The third congress of the Partido Comunista de Cuba in 1986 demonstrated the historical consistency of the Cuban Revolution by facing up to its own shortcomings in the context of the 1980s, but the critical evaluation of errors had not yet reached its most profound and comprehensive expression. By the middle of the 1980s it was clear that the implementation of economic policy and the mechanisms associated with it had generated some negative results in relation to the strategic objectives that should have been achieved by Cuban socialist society. From the end of 1985 on there were increasing complaints about health services (especially in the capital), obvious violations of salary policy due to the large number of profit-making activities that developed beginning with the enactment of the housing law, and irregularities in the operations of agricultural production cooperatives, especially in their relation to peasant free markets. On April 19, 1986, at the commemoration of the twenty-fifth anniversary of the victory at the Bay of Pigs, Fidel Castro denounced these shortcomings and the serious deficiencies that were apparent in the policy mechanisms used to direct the country's economy. It can be said that this event marked the beginning of the rectification process. From this point on it was evident that the economic and social policies used for the construction of socialism in Cuba would have to change and that this process would require a complex and multifaceted approach and a long period of time for its implementation.

The causes of the distortion detected in the mid-1980s were multiple and complex. "Among the most important were weak administration, indolence and tolerance within union structures, and serious weaknesses in political work" (PCC, 1986:144). Regarding the last point, Fidel Castro's comments stand out: "The Party at a certain moment was dedicated to its internal life and other tasks, ignoring the economy. The Party itself, I believe, developed a negative tendency" (Castro, 1988:264). More generally, it can be said that the experiences of other socialist countries had been assimilated uncritically, without the necessary adjustments to fit the Cuban reality, because no political evaluation of the economic processes fundamental to socialism took place.

The most serious error of the economic policy put in practice between 1976 and 1985 was undoubtedly its reliance upon economic mechanisms to resolve all the problems faced by a new society, ignoring the role assigned to political factors in the construction of socialism (Castro, 1987:13). The highest levels of the Party had warned about these problems even as the new system of economic management was being approved in 1975. Regarding this point it was stressed that "no system under socialism can substitute for the role of ideology, the conscience of the people, because the factors that determine efficiency in the capitalist economy are and continue to be the political, ideological, and normative aspects, which are fundamental and decisive—and cannot exist in any form under socialism" (PCC, 1978:113).

Additionally, errors were committed in implementing economic policy by assigning priority to material incentives (premiums) and paying insufficient attention to the controls and penalties (fines) that would have created an adequate balance between the mechanisms of stimulation and those of management control. From a broad point of view, a progressive disproportion was observed between growth in terms of value, on the one hand, and a decline in the availability of use values, on the other. In practice the system promoted the measuring of economic efficiency almost exclusively on the basis of profit, which motivated enterprises to give priority to the activities that were most profitable without considering their social utility. Thus, while the construction industry grew (in terms of value) at an average annual rate of 9.3 percent between 1981 and 1985, 28 percent of the investments were classified as ongoing (*en proceso*), that is to say, investments that did not mature during that period (CEE, 1987a:111; González and Pico, 1987:13). The unbalanced growth of the economy was also evident in the increased foreign trade deficit, which tripled during these five years, worsening the country's financial difficulties.

Moreover, during this time there was an increase in work productivity alongside a deterioration in the effective use of basic assets (*fondos básicos*), which declined from 59 percent in 1980 to 54 percent in 1985 (CEE, 1987a:101, 170).[1] At the management level, serious problems occurred over violations of the principle of payment commensurate with work. Above all, this began with the setting of excessively low work standards, which resulted in payments above what was considered socially necessary. From this developed corruption, wastefulness, and other negative consequences. Job standards in 1984 were in fact very questionable, 77 percent of them being classified as elementary. Moreover, the standards set in 1980 were surpassed, averaging 110 percent and rising to 117.6 percent in 1986. All of this contributed to a growth in the mean monthly salary from 148 pesos in 1980 to 188 pesos in 1985, while during this time monetary liquidity in the population rose by 867 million pesos (CTC, 1984:216; Flores, 1984:107; Lafite, 1987:9; CEE, 1987a:173–174).

Imbalances produced by errors were also manifested in the social sphere, particularly in sectors such as education, health care, and housing. From 1980 to 1985, for example, only twelve child care centers were constructed in the country, even though by mid-1982 demand (primarily in Havana) surpassed by twenty thousand the available places (CEE, 1987a:52). The lack of child care facilities created serious difficulties for the incorporation into the work force of women, who by then represented 38 percent of workers and 56.4 percent of technicians (FMC, n.d.:24).

In the field of health care, the availability of hospital facilities declined. Thus, the number of patients per bed went from 175.2 in 1970 to 192.9 by 1985. A greater deterioration was observed in Havana, where the patient-per-bed index rose from 82.3 to 102.1 in the same period (calculation based on CEE, 1987a:61, 577).

One of the most striking social indicators of problems, however, was housing construction. The housing deficit went from an estimated 754,800 dwellings in 1970 to 888,000 in 1985, with the most critical situation in Havana and Santiago (Economía y Desarrollo, 1988:118).

The errors committed in the operation of the economy and the social tensions that ensued had serious repercussions both ideologically and politically. The erroneous use of material incentives stimulated an increase in individual interests as opposed to the communal interests of the entire society (PCC, 1986:144). The rise of individualism was seen in the actions of speculators and middlemen—including workers—who enriched themselves on the margins of society. Administrators began to use commercial management methods, paying workers high wages that were out of proportion to their output. Bureaucrats developed a technocratic approach to economic problems that entirely underestimated the political and social impact of their decisions. All these phenomena encouraged an increase in criminal activity and disrespect for socialist law. The economic mechanisms implemented contributed to the erosion of the foundations of social property by distorting collective ownership of the means of production.

In general, economic policy after 1976 contained errors attributable to economism and commercialism and, contrary to what had occurred at the end of the 1960s, did not advance development. Instead it retarded the advancement of socialism as a system and threatened the realization of its strategic objectives. The multiplicity of problems made it apparent that, though some of the causes were of long standing, many were recent. This led the leaders of the revolution to insist on adequate reflection with regard to all policies to ensure that errors and negative tendencies not be repeated. Consequently, throughout 1986 one notes a process of investigation to determine the magnitude of the errors and what measures were necessary to overcome them. At the same time, steps began to be taken to correct errors and distortions, a process that extended throughout 1987. Also, from 1986 on economic and social policies were oriented toward searching for new mechanisms that would allow the correction of errors and create the basis of a new system of economic management in line with the objective of constructing socialism in Cuba (see Castro, 1988).

Economic and Social Measures, 1986–1989

The first decisions were made in the economic sphere with a series of documents that rescinded existing policy (CETSS, 1986, 1987, 1988). These documents concentrated on salary and work organization, particularly regarding the standardization of work, salary structures, priority systems, staff sizes, and work qualifications. Among the changes were a revision of production standards, a reduction in the number of job titles alongside an increase in responsibilities, layoffs, and a revision of salary structures. The changes also sought to debureaucratize state management, improve the quality of statistical and accounting data, and increase the effectiveness of economic controls. Systems of planning, economic controls, supply, investment, labor and salary policy, quality control, contracting, and secondary production were all affected.

Among the most significant measures was the elimination in May 1986 of the peasant free markets. This free-market mechanism, created in April 1980, had deformed the process of agricultural cooperativization, encouraged the development of ideologies incompatible with socialism on the part of small peasants, and stimulated the rapid rise of middlemen and speculators (see CEE, 1987a:394; Castro, 1986:55). All this promoted an unjust redistribution of income in favor of socially unproductive groups, with negative social and political repercussions.[2] Also in May 1986, Decree-Law No. 92 designated responsibilities for directors, functionaries, and even workers for their own management. In like manner, measures aimed at eliminating incorrect procedures were enacted, and limitations were established on the practice of self-employment in 1986.[3] In July of that year the Comisión Nacional del Sistema de Dirección de la Economía (CNSDE) was created to study proposed changes to the economic system and to overcome the noted shortcomings (see CNSDE, 1988a, 1988b, 1988c). In 1987 the regulations for the formation of premium assets (*fondos de premio*) were left intact.[4] Also in 1987, gratuities for dining services and worker transports were eliminated. Finally, in 1988 a regulation was enacted to establish adequate procedures in relation to employment levels within enterprises.[5] This led to a restructuring of the Ministry of Basic Industry that reduced the administrative personnel in its central offices by 60 percent and to a regulated employment policy (*Prensa Latina*, December 24, 1988).

At the same time, measures were implemented to correct obvious shortcomings in economic management. In 1987 the minimum salary was raised to 100 pesos per month, benefiting 186,000 health care workers, 13,700 bakery workers, and more than 200,000 agricultural laborers, and in 1988 the summer wage rate was raised for agricultural workers. All these measures were implemented without change in the national mean monthly salary, which was 188 pesos in 1985 and 187 pesos in 1988 (CEE, 1987a:174; 1988:7).

A new form of work first materialized in construction with the creation of the Blas Roca Contingent in October 1987. This type of labor collective, in which the communist work ethic is combined with socialist compensation, has produced extraordinary results in the areas to which it was assigned, achieving a high level of economic efficiency. At the end of 1988 the contingent consisted of 1,280 workers who worked an average of 13.2 hours a day throughout the year, reaching a productivity of 16,004 pesos, with the cost per peso of output being 77 centavos, and yielding an average salary of 315 pesos per month (Barro, 1988:7). This style of work was gradually extended throughout the country during 1988 and by mid-1989 included 61 contingents with 20,000 workers (*Trabajadores*, July 31, 1989).

Thus the rectification process has been effective in modifying essential elements of economic policy in order to establish more efficient management. Accordingly, by September 1988, half a million of a total of three million work norms were eliminated and a 65 percent reduction in job titles was achieved (*Trabajadores*, September 10, 1988), all without increasing unemployment—calculated at 6 percent of the economically active population since 1985 (see Castro, 1985:33; Mayra Lavigne, cited in *Caribbean Insight*, February 1989)—or the average salary. Moreover, in work collectives where new management criteria were applied, efficiency increased; in 1988 the Blas Roca Contingent achieved a productivity rate 2.12 times greater than that of the construction sector in 1985 (calculations based on Barro, 1988; CEE, 1987a:195).

In the social sphere the rectification process also immediately made itself felt. To solve problems in the area of basic social services, attention was given to accelerating construction to meet the needs for child care centers, health installations, and housing, particularly in Havana. A decisive step in this direction was taken in September 1986 with the reactivation of the microbrigades, whose objectives included performing social tasks as well as constructing housing. In the first two years of their operation the microbrigades built 110 child care centers with a capacity for more than twenty-three thousand children (25 percent above the projected needs in 1986), practically solving the problem (Castro, 1989:1).

Additionally, by September 1989 the microbrigades had constructed 16,515 dwellings, 1,657 family medical clinics, 22 bakeries, 9 polyclinics, 8 special-education schools, the EXPOCUBA, and the Robotic Center, along with various other projects (*Granma*, October 2, 1989). Consequently, important shortages in basic social services were filled, particularly in the area of health care. Among the brigades' most significant projects in 1988 were the expansion of the Miguel Enríquez Hospital, with a capacity of 300 beds, the expansion of the Frank País Orthopedic Hospital, and the construction of a center for ocular microsurgery, with a daily capacity of 1,200 patients. In all, medical-care beds rose from 52,643 in 1985 to 59,720 in 1988, with the population-per-bed ratio dropping from 192.9 to 175.3. During the same period the number of social-care beds grew from 11,517 to 13,172.

Microbrigades composed of housekeepers, retirees, students, and workers on overtime not only constructed houses but also systematically repaired and maintained those in poor condition. They had a rationalizing impact on these sectors of the work force and generated encouraging results for socialism by linking the organized effort of the population to development programs and to the solution of problems most directly affecting them.

Other measures adopted to overcome deficiencies in the social sphere included a new housing law in December 1988 that corrected the errors of the 1984 law. In the area of social security, pensions were increased in January 1987, benefiting more than 725,000 people. In general, the resources directed by the state to cover basic social services increased between 1985 and 1988 by 7.3 percent in housing and communal services and 12.1 percent in public education and health (Banco Nacional de Cuba, 1987b:17; 1989a:12).

The rectification process begun in 1986 will involve a search for solutions to complex problems that have not been satisfactorily resolved in other socialist countries. In this process the Cuban Revolution has been true to the principles that it considers essential to the construction of socialism, whereby economic, political, and social aspects form an indivisible unity and the development of revolutionary consciousness plays a fundamental role.

The Evolution of the Cuban Economy in the 1980s

The development of the Cuban economy from 1981 through 1985 took place under especially complicated circumstances. From the internal point of view, errors were made in the implementation of economic policy that

precipitated unbalanced growth and the appearance of serious disequi-
libria, especially between the economic and social spheres, in the development process. Additionally, the adverse climatic conditions that had
caused so much damage during the preceding five-year period intensified.
Particularly destructive were the drought beginning in May 1983 and
Hurricane Kate at the end of 1985.[6]

The international capitalist economic situation was also highly unfavorable. In addition to the negative consequences of the international
economic crisis between 1980 and 1982 were the tightening of the North
American economic blockade and the decline of sugar prices, both of
which had already negatively affected Cuba at the end of the 1970s and
required renegotiation of service payments (in freely convertible currency)
on the foreign debt accumulated since the end of 1982.

Despite all this, the industrialization of the country continued to be
the focus of economic development strategy. Except for the agricultural
sector, which was negatively affected by adverse weather, and the transportation and communication sectors, which were more sensitive to unfavorable foreign conditions, the economy showed positive performance
in terms of value in the first half of the 1980s compared with the preceding
five-year period. This performance was achieved, however, on the basis
of a pattern of extensive growth characterized by loss of efficiency of
basic assets, especially in industry,[7] accumulation of inventories, and
ongoing investments (Unanue and Martínez, 1989:71–72). At the management level, the setting of excessively low standards of work resulted
in pay beyond that considered socially necessary, and this contributed to
an extraordinary growth in the mean monthly salary at a time when
monetary liquidity in the population was rising.

Finally, the unbalanced growth of the economy manifested itself in the
increased trade deficit, magnifying the country's financial difficulties. The
deteriorating terms of trade, which was estimated around 21 percent for
the period, had a determinant effect on this outcome.[8] The adverse
international financial situation also had an impact. During the first half
of the 1980s debt service in freely convertible currency rose to 3.745
billion pesos, which represented 56.7 percent of the value of exports for
this period (Rodríguez, 1987:18).

In general, this period saw a certain level of economic and social
development but not the level that might have been achieved with the
efficient utilization of the available resources.

During the three-year period 1986–1989 the economy showed an even
more complex evolution. It was impossible to ignore the accumulated
effects of the errors committed in the operation of the economy during
the 1976–1985 period or the imbalance in the development process that
those errors had engendered, but the economic results obtained between

1986 and 1988 were also significantly affected by negative external factors brought about by the adverse international capitalist economic situation that had characterized the first half of the 1980s. Because of the decline of petroleum prices[9] during 1986, income in freely convertible currency was reduced abruptly by an amount equivalent to 320 million pesos, to which was added a loss of 120 million pesos due to the devaluation of the dollar (Banco Nacional de Cuba, 1987b:4). When the losses due to the unfavorable weather conditions are added to the above, the total drop of foreign-currency income is estimated at 600 million pesos in a single year, balanced against an estimated minimum of 1.6 billion pesos of necessary imports, payable in freely convertible currency (Banco Nacional de Cuba, 1987b:3, 15).

This situation created severe tensions for the country's foreign financing that caused the postponement of debt service payment in July 1986. Cuba requested renegotiation of the previous payment agreements of 1983, 1984, and 1985 and of those that ought to have occurred in 1986 and 1987. A proposal was made to amortize the previous debts over a term of twelve years, including a six-year grace period. Additionally, Cuba requested fresh credits to cover the net currency loss generated by the new international situation, totaling some 430 million pesos (Banco Nacional de Cuba, 1986b:16–19; Ritter, 1988). However, these proposals were not accepted, and the renegotiation of the Cuban debt within the framework of the Paris Club remained stalled until September 1989.[10] The freezing of loans that this produced entailed the need to renegotiate short-term credit for current trade beginning in the summer of 1986, creating a very complex situation for the management of foreign trade.

The foreign financial situation that confronted the country meant that its debt in freely convertible currency would rise from 3.621 billion pesos in 1985 to 6.45 billion pesos in 1988 (Banco Nacional de Cuba, 1987b:41; 1989a:38). However, of this increase new credit amounted to only 376.7 million pesos, which represented 13.3 percent of the total increase, between 1986 and 1989.[11] Moreover, the changes in the exchange rates also raised the level of the debt. Consequently, beginning in 1987 Cuba devalued the peso from $1.20 to $1.00 to the peso, which increased the nominal debt by 1.062 billion pesos, representing 37.5 percent of the total debt increase in this period (Banco Nacional de Cuba, 1987c:7). Similarly, the movements of the exchange rates of the dollar to other freely convertible currencies caused an estimated increase in the Cuban foreign debt between 1987 and 1988 of 767.8 million pesos, which represented 27.1 percent of the total debt increase from 1986 to 1988.[12]

The severe foreign financial restrictions required the adoption of a plan, which included twenty-seven measures, intended to raise the level of savings in the country (*Granma*, December 27, 1986). Beginning in 1986 the Cuban economy was overcome by the combined effects of the adverse international economic situation and the errors made in the management of the economy in previous years. The country faced a difficult and protracted process of redirecting the economy during a period of difficult relations with the developed capitalist countries and accelerating transformation in the socialist international division of labor.

Given these internal and external conditions, Cuba has since 1986 faced contraction in a number of areas favorable to development. The net accumulation rate fell from 23.3 percent in 1985 to 16.2 percent in 1986 and then to 11.9 percent in 1987, with a recovery planned to reach levels of 17–18 percent in 1988 (CEE, 1987a:101, 215; Banco Nacional de Cuba, 1989a:4, *La Nación Cubana*, no. 14, 1988). This decline was explained by a policy of rationalization that sought to complete previously initiated projects in order to ensure their contribution to the development of the country. At the same time, external limitations also influenced this decline. The indicators that measure the efficiency of productive management at the macro-level were also seriously affected. Work productivity fell 1.5 percent in 1986, 6.1 percent in 1987, and 1.7 percent in 1988. The efficiency of the basic productive assets declined from 54.4 percent in 1985 to 40.4 percent in 1987 (calculations based on CEE, 1987a:135, 171, 195; Banco Nacional de Cuba, 1989b:4). From the internal point of view, the economy was also negatively impacted by the continuation of unfavorable climatic conditions such as irregular rainfall, which affected the agricultural sector and especially sugar production.

The overall economy showed a clear period of contraction until 1987, followed by a modest recovery in 1988 resulting in production levels very close to those existing in 1985. All sectors except construction and trade showed growth relative to 1985 (Table 8.1). Sugar production recovered its 1985 levels in 1988, reaching 7.8 million tons, although from 1985 to 1987 the adverse weather conditions had caused a drop in output (Banco Nacional de Cuba, 1989b:11; CEE, 1987a:248).

It is necessary to add the impact of foreign trade to the financial atmosphere and external conditions that influenced the evolution of the country's economy during this period. In general, the overall trade deficit in 1988 remained at the 1985 level but with a decrease in freely convertible currencies and an increase in currency from socialist countries. Exports to countries trading with convertible currencies grew 14.0 percent while exports to socialist countries declined 10.5 percent. This decline was largely due to the drop in sugar production and the decline in sugar exports, which went from 4.7 million tons in 1985 to 4.3 million tons in 1988 (Banco Nacional de Cuba, 1987b:22; 1989a:23). Imports payable in convertible currencies contracted by 24.6 percent between 1985 and 1988 and settled at a level equivalent to 59.6 percent of the estimated minimum

TABLE 8.1   Production Levels, 1985 and 1988

Product	1985	1988
Vegetables (thousand metric tons)	584.2	675.6
Citrus (thousand metric tons)	747.5	976.4
Electricity (thousand kilowatt hours)	12.2	14.5
Processed crude petroleum (thousand metric tons)	6,587.3	7,642.6
Natural gas (million cubic meters)	6.9	21.9
Recycled chromium (thousand metric tons)	37.7	52.2
Compound piping (units)	606.0	642.0
Buses (units)	2,393.0	2,537.0
Grey cement (million metric tons)	3.2	3.6
Cloth (million square meters)	205.4	260.1
Clothing (million units)	51.8	61.2
Fresh poultry (thousand metric tons)	67.0	73.8
Fish (thousand metric tons)	219.9	231.6

Sources: Banco Nacional de Cuba (1987a:7–11; 1989b:8–12).

imports required, which had strong repercussions on the economic recovery of the country. Imports from the socialist countries also dropped 1.4 percent. However, tourism has partially compensated for the foreign trade deficit. During 1985, 240,500 tourists produced 100.4 million pesos in foreign-currency income, while 309,200 tourists in 1988 generated income of 152.9 million pesos in foreign currency (Banco Nacional de Cuba, 1987a:19; 1989a:9; Martín, 1988).

Finally, it is appropriate to remember that the period from 1986 to 1988 was also marked by a process of profound change in economic and social policy that, although it undoubtedly had a favorable impact on the recovery, clearly complicated matters. The changes in economic policy beginning in 1986 were directed at guaranteeing an equilibrium between economic factors and the sociopolitical factors that ought to be realized in a process of socialist development. They were aimed in part at reducing the foreign trade deficit through selective investment in scarce disposable resources with the intention of obtaining a higher rate of recovery from the same foreign convertible currency. The determinants of the evolution of the Cuban economy between 1986 and 1989 included the unfavorable effects of the adverse international economic situation, the consequent absence of foreign financing in terms of freely convertible currencies, and the negative impact of the errors in economic policy and in the system of directing the economy.[13] The results achieved by the Cuban economy through 1988 exhibited a trend toward recovery approaching 1985 levels, but the growth achieved was essentially extensive and its level of efficiency was limited by external factors and internal conditions.[14] The preliminary results of the first eight months of 1989 and the prognosis that can be made in relation to possible economic growth for the year indicate the same tendencies in 1988.[15] Thus growth of 1.5 percent is expected for the Cuban economy for 1989.[16] To complete this prognosis, accumulated growth from 1985 through 1989 will be 0.9 percent. Despite the difficulties confronted in this period, the level of fulfillment of social needs rose with minimal impact on the population's level of consumption.

Notes

1. Effectiveness in the use of basic assets is calculated as a comparison between the growth of these assets and the growth of national income.

2. Reported sales in the peasant free markets came to represent only about 1 percent of commercial retail circulation and in 1985 generated income of 70 million pesos (CEE, 1987b:394; Castro, 1986:55).

3. At the end of 1987 there were 28,839 self-employed workers registered in the country (see Estrategias de Nairobi, 1989:41).

4. The payment for premium assets dropped from 90.5 million pesos in 1985 to 87.8 million pesos in 1986, 52.3 million pesos in 1987, and 45.4 million pesos in 1988 (CEE, 1987b:116; 1989a:120).

5. In 1988 a decrease of 6,300 administrative workers and 16,400 managers was reported (*Granma*, December 16, 1988).

6. Up to 1986, the accumulated effects of the two events generated losses of 1,240,000 metric tons of sugar, with a value of $160 million (Banco Nacional de Cuba, 1987b:3).

7. The effective use of basic assets in industry fell from 57.7 percent in 1980 to 49.3 percent in 1985 (CEE, 1985:136, 166).

8. These estimates are based on calculations from a sample representing 60 percent of imports and 80 percent of exports (Fernández and Pico, 1988:11).

9. The reexport of petroleum supplied by the Soviet Union provided 509 million pesos between 1983 and 1985 and represented 42 percent of income in freely convertible currency in the latter year (Banco Nacional de Cuba, 1986a:23).

10. The official creditors agreed to postpone the 1986 payment of $116 million of the principal and to consider later the payment for 1987, offering fresh credit of 75 million pesos. However, the commercial banks proposed to lend an additional $85 million for one year and provide commercial lines of credit for $600 million and to restructure the $75 million due in 1986 to be paid in ten years with a six-year grace period. Since the conditions imposed by the private creditors differed greatly from what Cuba had requested, no accord was reached (Ritter, 1988; *Cuba Business*, April 1987). The Cubans maintained that it would be impossible for the country to meet the conditions for covering the debt without fresh credit, while the creditors demanded a profound restructuring of the Cuban economy as a guarantee for the authorization of such credit.

11. The net credit received in 1986 was 249.4 million pesos; in 1987 it was 84.8 million and in 1988 only 42.5 million (Banco Nacional de Cuba, 1987b:28; 1988:21; 1989a:19).

12. In 1987 the debt increased in the same manner by 299.8 million pesos; in 1988 short-term credit rose only 42.5 percent (Banco Nacional de Cuba, 1988:22; 1989a:18–19).

13. Other historical factors also influenced the socioeconomic structure inherited by the country in 1959 and the errors committed in the management of the Cuban economy in the first years of the revolution.

14. For example, monetary liquidity grew by 537.9 million pesos from 1986 to 1988, and to this was added an accumulated budgetary deficit of 1.943 billion pesos in the same period (Banco Nacional de Cuba, 1987b:15; 1988:12, 15; 1989a:11–12).

15. During the first eight months of 1989 investments grew 13.2 percent and construction increased 6.7 percent compared with the same period in 1988. Commercial retail circulation rose 4.1 percent and the mean salary 1.1 percent. At the same time, industrial production declined 0.6 percent, agricultural production 4.1 percent, communications 2.9 percent, and work productivity 4.0 percent (CEE, 1989b:16, 52, 59, 60, 110, 112, 128). Sugar production reached 8,124,320 metric tons for an increase of 9.6 percent over the previous harvest (*Granma*, June 2, 1989).

16. This figure is my estimate on the basis of various projections developed in Cuba.

References

Banco Nacional de Cuba. 1986a. *Informe Económico* (March). Havana.

_____. 1986b. *Balanza de pagos perspectivas para 1986–1987.* Havana.

_____. 1987a. *Información estadística seleccionada de la economía cubana.* Havana.

_____. 1987b. *Informe Económico* (May). Havana.

_____. 1987c. *Informe Económico* (September). Havana.

_____. 1988. *Informe Económico* (June). Havana.

_____. 1989a. *Informe Económico* (May). Havana.

_____. 1989b. *Información estadística seleccionada sobre la economía cubana.* Havana.

Barro, Emilio del. 1988. "Contingente Blas Roca Calderio: Germina potente semilla." *Granma* (December 31).

Brundenius, Claes. 1984. *Revolutionary Cuba: The Challenge of Economic Growth with Equity.* Boulder: Westview.

Castro, Fidel. 1985. *Fidel y la religión: Conversaciones con Frei Betto.* Havana: Publicaciones del Consejo de Estado.

_____. 1986. "En el Encuentro Nacional de Cooperativas de Producción Agropecuario." *Cuba Socialista* (23).

_____. 1987. "Discurso pronunciado en la clausula del V Congreso de la Unión de Jóvenes Comunistas, La Habana 5 de abril de 1987." *Cuba Socialista* (27).

_____. 1988. "Diálogo sostenido con los participantes en el III Congreso de la Asociación de Economistas de América Latina y el Caribe, La Habana 23 al 26 de noviembre de 1987," in *Por el camino correcto,* 2d ed. Havana: Editoria Política.

_____. 1989. "Discurso del Comandante en Jefe Fidel Castro en el Acto por el tercer anniversario de la revitalización del movimiento de microbrigadistas, 30 de septiembre 1989." *Granma* (October 2).

CEE (Comité Estatal de Estadísticas). 1985. *Anuario Estadístico de Cuba.* Havana.

_____. 1987a. *Anuario Estadístico de Cuba.* Havana.

_____. 1987b. *Boletín Estadístico de Cuba.* Havana.

_____. 1988. *La economía cubana.* Havana.

_____. 1989a. *Boletín Estadística de Cuba* (January–March). Havana.

_____. 1989b. *Boletín Estadística de Cuba* (January–August). Havana.

CETSS (Comité Estatal de Trabajo y Seguridad Social). 1986. *Plan de acción contra las irregularidades administrativas y los errors debilidades del sistema de dirección de la economía.* Havana.

_____. 1987. *Orientaciones a los organismos de la administración central del estado y a los Organos Locales del Poder Popular.* Havana.

_____. 1988. *Orientaciones a los organismos de la administración central del estado y a los Organos Locales del Poder Popular.* Havana.

CNSDE (Comisión Nacional del Sistema de Dirección de la Economía). 1988a. *Decisiones adoptadas sobre algunos elementos del sistema de la dirección de la economía 1* (March). Havana.

_____. 1988b. *Decisiones adoptadas sobre algunos elementos del sistema de la dirección de la economía 2* (June). Havana.

_____. 1988c. "Normas sobre la unión y las empresas estatales de subordinación nacional." *Cuba Economía Planificada* 4 (October–December).

CTC (Central de Trabajadores de Cuba). 1984. *XV Congreso de la CTC: Memorias.* Havana: Ciencias Sociales.

Economía y Desarrollo. 1988. "Población y fondo de viviendas, 1971–1985." 2 (March–April).

Estrategias de Nairobi. 1989. *Seminario "Difusión y Evolución de las Estrategias de Nairobi: Orientaciones hacia el futuro para promoción de la mujer—Empleo," Havana, 21 al 23 de noviembre 1989.*

Fernández, Mario, and Nieves Pico. 1988. *Consideraciones sobre la evolución de la industria y el sector externo de la economía cubana durante el período revolucionario.* Havana: INIE.

Flores, Barbara. 1984. "Breve análisis del sistema salarial actual en los marcos de la reforma general de salarios." *Revista Economía y Desarrollo* 78 (January–February).

FMC (Federación de Mujeres Cubanas). n.d. *Integración de la mujer cubana a las actividades socioeconómicas y políticas.* Havana: Editorial de la Mujer.

González, José E., and Nieves Pico. 1987. "Diagnóstico global del proceso inversionista en Cuba en el período 1975–84." *Compendio de Investigaciones* 1 (June).

Guevara, Ernesto Che. 1977. "El socialismo y el hombre en Cuba," in *Escritos y discursos,* vol. 8. Havana: Ciencias Sociales.

Lafite, Caridad. 1987. "La normación del trabajo: panorámica de un año." *Trabajadores* (August 13).

Martín, Ramón. 1988. "El turismo y su desarrollo." *Revista Economía y Desarrollo* 5 and 6.

Mesa-Lago, Carmelo. 1981. *The Economy of Socialist Cuba*. Albuquerque: University of New Mexico Press.

PCC (Partido Comunista de Cuba). 1978. *Primer Congreso del Partido Comunista de Cuba: Informe central*. Havana: Editorial Pueblo y Educación.

———. 1986. "II Pleno del Comité Central del Partido Comunista de Cuba: Analiza la máxima dirección del partido marcha de la economía y del proceso de rectificación de errores y tendencias negativas." *Cuba Socialista* (23).

Ritter, A. R. 1988. "El problema de la deuda de Cuba en monedas convertibles." *Revista de CEPAL* 36 (December).

Rodríguez, José Luis. 1984. *Dos ensayos sobre economía cubana*. Havana: Ciencias Sociales.

———. 1987. "El desarrollo de Cuba en el contexto de la crisis económica latinoamericano de los años 80." *Temas de Economía Mundial* 19.

———. 1989. "El desarrollo económico y social de Cuba: resultados de 30 años de revolución." *Cuba Socialista* (39).

Unanue, A., and R. Martínez. 1989. "El desbalance financiero en el desarrollo de la economía cubana." *Cuba Economía Planificada* 3 (July-September).

Zimbalist, Andrew, and Susan Eckstein. 1987. "Patterns of Cuban development: The first twenty-five years," in Andrew Zimbalist (ed.), *Cuba's Socialist Economy: Towards the 1990s*. Boulder and London: Lynne Rienner.

9

Structural Changes in the Cuban Economy

Miguel Alejandro Figueras

Translated by Diana Alarcón and Terry McKinley

During the nineteenth century and particularly during the first three decades of the twentieth, the Cuban economy suffered from a major structural deformation. Its model of development, based on extreme specialization in sugar production, prevented growth in the rest of the economy and led to economic and political dependence on the United States.

At the beginning of the 1920s the new generation of Cuban youth understood that the country's economic structure condemned it to stagnation, imbalances, inequalities, defenselessness, and underdevelopment. The pressing need to diversify the economy was obvious to the best members of that generation. Many of the revolutionaries who struggled against the dictatorship of Gerardo Machado (1924–1933) and afterward against that of Fulgencio Batista knew that social change had to be more profound than the simple overthrow of these dictators.

The period of growth based on sugar production reached its peak at the beginning of the 1920s, and for almost forty years thereafter per capita income remained at the same level. The bankruptcy of this model of development was evident. During that period some foreign institutions and individuals were also convinced of the need for change. Any serious analysis of the complex and stagnating reality of the Cuban economy inevitably revealed the necessity of transformation.

When the reactionary forces, in league with the U.S. embassy, liquidated the "Government of a Hundred Days" after the overthrow of Machado, they designated a new puppet government that immediately requested an unofficial institution of the U.S. government, the Foreign Policy Association, to diagnose Cuba's problems and make recommendations. Within a few months this institution supplied its analysis: It was considered impossible to develop Cuba with the structure that had been imposed on it during the preceding three decades:

> One of the surprising paradoxes of the history of Cuba is that, as a consequence of its struggle to achieve independence in 1895, the country lost control over its economic resources.
> In the first place, this system has demonstrated itself to be unstable in the highest degree, and it is difficult, if not impossible, to build a normal society in a country that depends almost exclusively on a product whose quantity and price are subject to great fluctuations. (Foreign Policy Association, 1934)

This analysis was correct in certain respects, but the solutions recommended by the Foreign Policy Association were insufficient and carefully avoided affecting the forces behind the economic structure. The Cuban government was even less interested in implementing the recommendations, and therefore, with the exception of the analysis itself and the formidable compilation of information, the report became a relic.

Fifteen years later, with the exhaustion of the factors that had kept sugar prices high, the Cuban government applied for a $200 million loan from the then-new World Bank (International Bank for Reconstruction and Development, IBRD), and this financial institution sent a mission to examine the conditions of the Cuban economy. That institution found the distorted Cuban economy completely nonfunctional:

> The Cuban economy confronts as much a problem as an opportunity. Its problem is to reduce its dependence on sugar, not by means of producing less sugar but rather by developing new enterprises. . . .
> The choice facing the Cuban people is clear. They can take advantage of the present opportunity to replace a stagnant economy dependent on only one product with a growing, dynamic, and diversified economy. This can result in a long and arduous task. It will imply great efforts and the sacrifice of traditions and control. (IBRD, 1951)

In 1951 Henry C. Wallich offered a detailed analysis—done before the World Bank study—of the impossibility of escaping the stagnation caused by Cuba's structure:

> Sugar dominates the political economy, and all other interests are subordinated to the interests of sugar. An example of this is Cuba's trade relations

with the United States, through which Cuban tariff concessions of significant magnitude have obstructed the possibilities of national industry. This has been the price Cuba has had to pay for a reasonable share of the United States sugar market. This tendency of the dominant interest to perpetuate itself leads to a vicious circle from which it is difficult to escape. (Wallich, 1951)

Even though there was some agreement on the need to modify the structure of the economy, to diversify it, to overcome its dependence on sugar production and build a more self-sufficient economy, there was obviously no agreement on how to do it. Those who did not choose or did not recognize the need to root out the causes of the distortion proposed actions that diverted attention toward other factors.

Fidel Castro's self-defense in his trial for the assault on the Moncada barracks described the measures the Cuban revolutionaries deemed necessary under the circumstances to break out of the vicious circle of stagnation, and the practical introduction of those measures started in 1959. In May of that year, in Buenos Aires, Castro explained how the revolutionary government conceived of the interrelation between agricultural and industrial transformation: "Thus, we have reached the conclusion in our country that the Agrarian Reform is essential to our industrial development, and in addition because the extraordinary number of unemployed can only be occupied by having them produce for those who work in the factories and in turn having those who work in factories produce for the workers in the countryside" (Castro, 1959).

The point of departure for these proposed changes was an economy in which one-third of national income depended on sugar production. Only 2 million hectares were being cultivated, but two-thirds of them were sugarcane plantations. Sugar constituted 80 percent of Cuba's exports. At the same time, 30 percent of the labor force was unemployed or seriously underemployed.

Although economic transformation has encompassed all sectors and branches of the economy, this chapter will focus on four areas: agriculture, industry, construction, and foreign trade.

Transforming a Backward Agriculture

In 1958 the value added in agriculture (560 million pesos) was distributed as follows: The sugarcane sector produced 45 percent, the livestock sector one-fifth, and nonsugar agriculture a little more than one-third. In order to maintain the extensive but low-yielding cattle production, 4.5 million hectares were given over to natural pastures—cultivated pastures were almost nonexistent. The rest of the livestock industry was poorly developed. Egg production was low, as was the production of pork for the domestic fresh-meat market. Even though milk consumption per capita was low, Cuba imported significant quantities of sweetened and condensed milk, cheese, and butter. In order to transform this situation—a typical example of plantation agriculture, distorted, traditional, and backward—it has been necessary to make large investments in infrastructure and training.

Nowadays there are about 330,000 people working in nonsugar agriculture and livestock production, 12,000 of whom have college degrees and more than 50,000 of whom have technical or precollege training (CEE, 1988). Investment in nonsugar agriculture and livestock production has accounted for one-fifth of total investment in the last thirty years. As a consequence, the agricultural picture has changed considerably, with production increasing by several times (Figure 9.1). Low levels of production persist, however, in coffee, tobacco, and cattle. The latter has been substantially improved from the point of view of the quality of the stock. Milking cows that used to average two liters a day now produce more than six. By 1967 the number of head had increased to 7 million, but at present the national herd has declined to just under 5 million. The principal reason has been the lack of balanced cattle feed. The solution to this problem is being sought in the development of sugarcane derivatives and the transformation of a good part of the 2 million hectares of natural pastures into cultivated ones, which can yield three to four times more food per unit of land.

Agriculture has been one of the sectors in which a number of structural and technical changes have been made. The sector employs seventy-five thousand tractors with a total of 5.5 million horsepower (formerly there were only nine thousand tractors); 1.8–1.9 million tons of fertilizers are being applied (in contrast to 200,000 tons before); and 22 percent of the land is now irrigated.

The current structure of net value added in agriculture has changed considerably in comparison with the situation in 1958: Sugarcane agriculture now produces 28 percent, nonsugar agriculture 37 percent, livestock 34 percent, agricultural services 1 percent (CEE, 1988).

The Process of Industrialization

In 1958 Cuban industry was made up of 2,000 enterprises, most of them artisan workshops employing fewer than ten workers. The 162 sugar refineries and another 100 enterprises were the only ones with more than one hundred workers. Within the nonsugar sector there was a subsector of relatively advanced technology, mostly made up of affiliates of U.S. and some European transnationals (oil, tires, glass, food, electricity, soaps

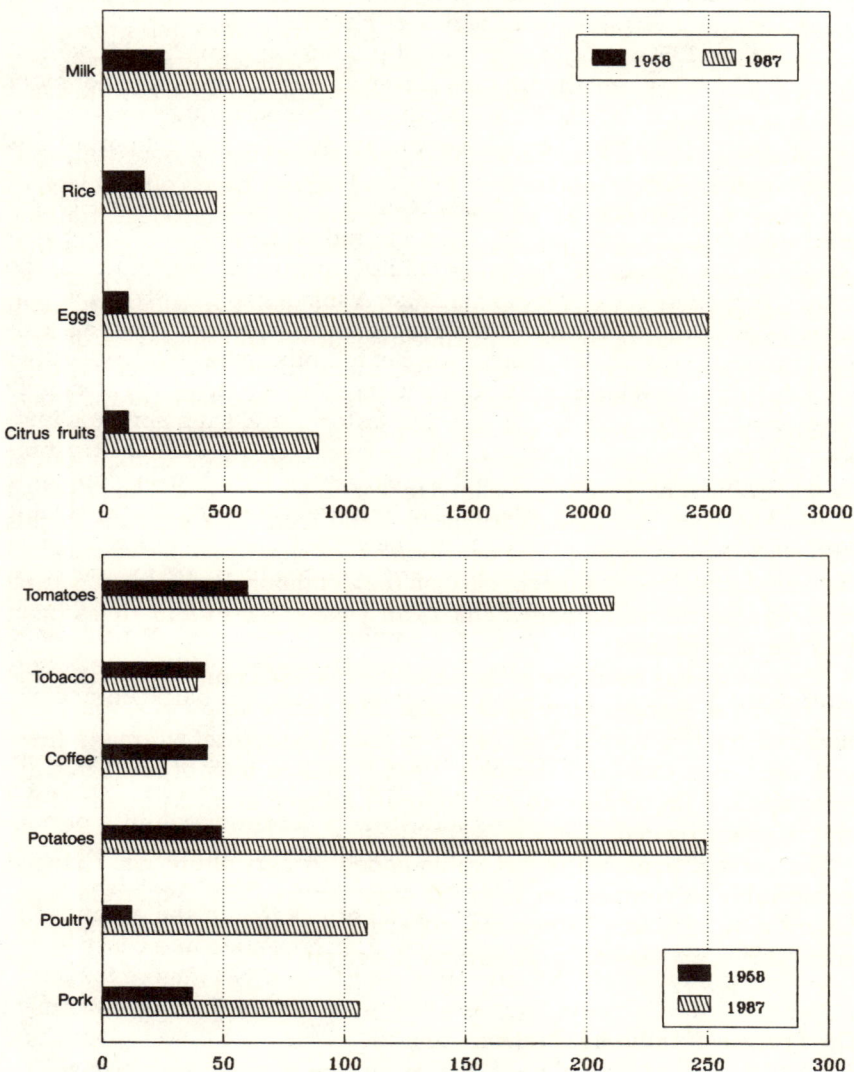

Figure 9.1 Nonsugar agricultural production (thousands of tons), 1958 and 1987 (CEE, n.d.; 1987; Ministerio de Hacienda, 1957).

and perfumes, etc.). Most of their inputs, parts, and equipment were imported. Nonsugar industrial employment was less than 10 percent of the total work force of the country, and 70 percent of its production was located within a fifty-kilometer radius of Havana.

During the 1950s nonsugar industrial production grew 2.5–2.9 percent a year. This modest growth rate was achieved with an investment of more than 600 million pesos facilitated by the great opportunities provided to foreign investors by the Cuban government. However, a great part of this industrial capacity remained unused.

From the beginning of the 1960s to the end of the 1980s, one-fourth of total investment was allocated to the industrial sector. During that period, as new stages of the industrialization process were reached, the objectives themselves underwent change. A major agroindustrial integration was achieved by means of the processing of food and other agricultural products (vegetables, fruits, rice, hemp, milk, pork, poultry, leather products), the establishment of a basic industry in fertilizers (formerly there were only mixing plants and one factory producing simple superphosphates, all close to Havana), the development of an industry producing sugarcane derivatives, and the rapid growth of industries supplying agricultural needs (feed, containers, wires, veterinary medicine). In the past, sectors producing capital goods, metal parts, and spares were practically nonexistent, except for a few large plants producing for the sugar industry and the railroads. Not counting simple repair shops classified as part of industry, the machine sector employed fewer than ten thousand workers. The development of these sectors during the 1960s was basically determined by the necessity of coping with the U.S. blockade and the goal of providing equipment to an expanding agriculture.

In the following years the economy continued to diversify and increase production. Today the machine, parts, and equipment sectors account for one-sixth of total nonsugar gross industrial production, one-fifth of nonsugar industrial employment, and one-fourth to one-third of investments in equipment. Industries such as steel and fishing, which once had a very low level of production, now play an important role in the economy. In others, such as pharmaceuticals, textiles, apparel, shoes, and construction materials, production levels have increased severalfold (Figure 9.2).

Industrial development required that an important part of investment in the sector be allocated to increasing the capacity of power plants, and this has permitted an eightfold increase in the generation of electricity.

In evaluating Cuban industrialization, it is necessary to take into account the following factors: The system of prices and tax collection considerably distorts the structural role of the industrial sector in aggregate figures. The low profit rates set in industry and the collection of indirect taxes through the commercial sector serve to inflate the proportion of

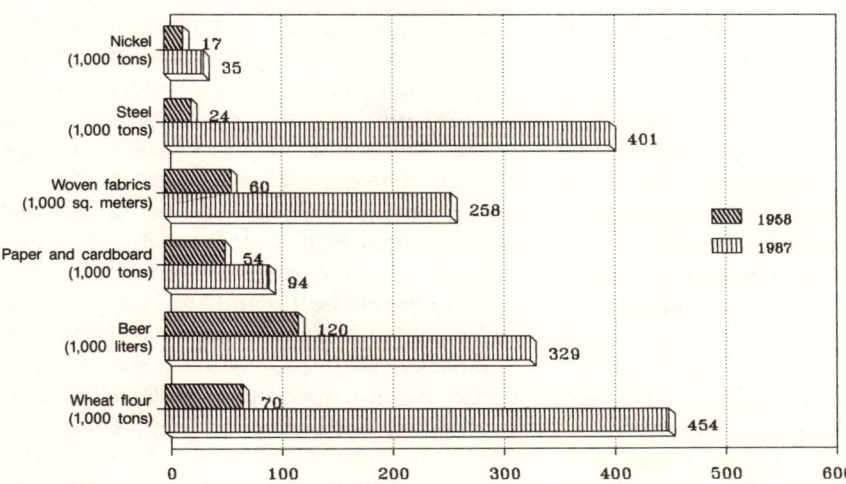

Figure 9.2   Nonsugar industrial production, 1958 and 1987 (CEE, n.d.; 1987).

TABLE 9.1   Participation in National Income (percentage) of Industry and Commerce, 1975 and 1987

	Uncorrected		Corrected[a]	
	1975	1987	1975	1987
Industry	47.8	46.7	48.7	55.5
Commerce	23.5	20.1	22.4	11.7

[a]Corrected figures take indirect taxation into account.

Sources: CEE (n.d.; 1987).

gross social product (GSP) of the latter at the expense of industry (Table 9.1). Eliminating the distortions derived from these factors, we find that the industrial sector accounts for more than half of national income. The percentage for industry would in fact be higher if the level of sugar production had not stagnated during the preceding years and if the industrial capacity in the nonsugar sector had been better utilized.

Furthermore, significant structural changes have taken place within the industrial sector; some industries have grown much more rapidly than others. Electronics, nonelectrical machinery, fish products, steel, and textiles and apparel, along with the generation of electricity, have grown at an annual rate of 9 percent during this period, contributing 30 percent of industrial production. At the same time, the share of sugar production in total industrial production has declined. Mineral production, which had a rapid rate of growth up until 1975, has decelerated in the last fifteen years, and this situation will not change until the new facilities for nickel production are in full operation. A similar deceleration of growth has been observed in the leather and food industries. With the exception of nitrogen fertilizers and pharmaceutical products (for human and veterinary uses), the chemical industry has not experienced significant growth. A contributing factor to this situation that must be rectified has been the lack of a petrochemical or alcohol-based chemical industry.

Finally, whenever possible, new industrial facilities have been located in provinces and regions with relatively little industrial development. This policy has been affected by forces working in the opposite direction—the benefits of economies of scale that exist in the more developed cities. Very often policy has been concerned with the expansion of existing factories, for example, in the nonintegrated steel and iron industry of the Havana area and in tire production. Additionally, there has been pressure to locate new industries close to the capital because of both the greater ease of administration and the greater confidence involved in locating new facilities where there is already an experienced work force. The consequence of this process has been a major decentralization of nonsugar production, and this has benefited other provinces even though appreciable disparities among them remain.

Changes in Investment and the Construction Industry

After the peak of investment in sugar production, railroad construction, and real estate—all of which were related to the expansion of the sugar industry during the first three decades of the century—construction activity declined abruptly and remained stagnant until the end of the 1940s and the early 1950s. Its recovery was attributable to housing and office construction as well as to government-sponsored public works programs. During this period the government implemented a policy known as "compensating expenditures," financed through an increase in the public debt, that was designed to counteract the decline of sugar exports. The supply of domestic inputs to construction was lacking, and therefore the growth of construction stimulated the growth of imports. The sector was heterogeneous, with little mechanization and no use of prefabricated material, and most of the planning of new factories, hotels, and similar complex projects was done by U.S. firms. Most projects (75–90 percent) were located in the old province of Havana. The sector gave employment to sixty-five thousand to seventy thousand workers.

The accelerated transformation of the agricultural sector required a modification in the geographical distribution of construction projects. The revolutionary state began to undertake its own construction projects, and by the end of the 1960s the most important construction companies had been nationalized. The effect of the blockade on spare parts supplied by

U.S. companies was felt with special force by the construction industry, particularly with regard to the maintenance of the few pieces of equipment used to build and maintain roads and highways. The stimulus provided by the growth of agricultural and road projects throughout the country increased the demand for this kind of equipment. (It was no coincidence that the first indemnification demanded by revolutionary Cuba from the U.S. government to compensate for the damage caused by the Bay of Pigs invasion took the form of bulldozers and other heavy equipment.)

Cuban engineers and architects had achieved relatively high levels of expertise in the construction of houses, offices, and occasionally hotels, but their experience in industrial projects was very limited. Highway construction techniques were not the best, and for maritime projects it was necessary to contract for the services of foreign companies.

The infrastructural weakness of the building materials industry called for rapid improvement. Two cement plants were contracted for and built during the first revolutionary decade, large quarry mills were acquired, the first prefabricated construction materials to be used were identified, and the first group of projects was organized.

The structure of the construction industry was substantially modified with the change in the sectoral and geographical allocation of investment. Agricultural and industrial investment, which represented only 32 percent of total investment in 1961, was increased to 60 percent. During 1966–1970 most of the construction effort was linked to the program of achieving 10 million tons of sugar by 1970. The absolute level of construction activity remained almost the same for the first ten years of the revolution, and profound structural change can be considered the principal feature of that period.

The five-year period 1971–1975 was characterized by very high rates of growth, construction becoming the most dynamic sector of the economy. Construction activity linked to education, agriculture, and industry grew the fastest during this period. Housing construction experienced a similar trend beginning halfway through this period when the newly created microbrigade movement gained momentum.

In the last fifteen years, 1975–1989, the composition of construction activity was altered, mainly in favor of industrial construction, roads, maintenance, and public health. Housing accounted for 10 percent of construction, and even though this level was higher than that of the 1960s it was still insufficient. Also during this period there was a serious lengthening of all construction projects, a loss of efficiency, a decrease in real productivity, and an inadequate distribution and use of materials and equipment. All of this required a reorganization of the sector at the beginning of the 1980s—changes in methods of work, a reestablishment of the microbrigades for housing construction, and an effort to utilize new forms of organization in the units. Geographically, construction was moved away from the city of Havana, where it had been concentrated, and spread throughout all the provinces.

It is not easy to compare past and present construction levels in value terms, but indices of the consumption of the principal building materials serve to illustrate the growth of construction. The 1987 indices for cement (400), stone (600), and sand (800), taking 1951–1955 consumption as 100, show the growth involved, which can be attributed equally to changes in the structure of projects and greater rationality in the use of materials.

Diversification of External Trade

It has been suggested that because sugar continues to represent a large proportion of total exports, there has been no structural transformation of Cuba's dependency on a single product. It seems simplistic, however, to focus on the percentage of sugar in total exports at current prices. During the 1950s the export of sugar and its derivatives represented 82 percent of the total. The share of tobacco exports had declined while the share of minerals increased because of the reopening and expansion of the Nicaro nickel plant, the increase in nickel exports compensating for the decline in the exports of copper, manganese, iron, and chromium. Fish exports were very limited.

After World War II there was an increase in exports of a group of products each of which in itself carried little weight but which together represented 8–9 percent of the total. Three-fourths of these were directed toward the United States and toward other Latin American countries. These exports were accomplished by various means and helped to create a network of microtrade relations over the years.

With commercial sanctions, the obstacles created by transnational corporations, and the sudden aggression represented by the trade blockade, the Cuban export system suffered heavy damage. The degree of effect varied with the product. Through the help of the Soviet Union and the other socialist countries it was possible to transfer sugar to those markets, and there was a similar development with minerals. It took a longer time to reorient the exports of tobacco and fish products, which had formerly been linked to the U.S. market and the markets of other Latin American countries, all of which except Mexico joined the blockade. Toward the end of the first decade of the revolution, exports of those products had been relocated, and fish exports had surpassed by several times their former levels.

Similar success was not enjoyed by the other group of Cuban products just mentioned. Because this second group involved thousands of products and because of the breakdown of Cuba's relations with its customers caused by the blockade, it was unable to regain the export levels it had attained in the 1960s. An analysis of fifteen products from this group whose exports in 1957 had earned 57 million pesos (total exports of the second group had earned 63 million pesos) shows that 80 percent of them were exported to the United States and Latin America. The principal effort against the blockade was focused on avoiding paralysis due to the lack of parts, energy, raw materials, and necessary foodstuffs. The pressure applied by the U.S. embassies on allied countries in Europe and Asia to prevent them from selling their products to Cuba, the blacklisting of ships bringing goods to Cuba, and many other measures created blockade mentality within the economy. Neutralizing these actions through institutional reorganization and the creation of a state system of external trade—until then nonexistent—demanded most of the attention of the political leadership, and all this played a role in explaining the low export levels of this second group of products.

This is why Cuban exports during the 1960s and part of the 1970s were 98 percent concentrated in sugar, minerals, tobacco, and fish products. Despite an aggressive policy of promoting and creating external markets, which multiplied by nearly twenty the export levels of these products during the ten years from 1965 to 1975, the second group of products did not return to its 1957 level of 50–60 million pesos until 1974–1975. The entrance into production since the mid-1970s of items designed for export, such as citrus products, and the emphasis on the promotion of nontraditional exports have resulted in a more than tenfold increase in the export of these goods in the subsequent years. Included in this group are exports of Cuban oil, naphtha, lubricants, and other products from national refineries but not the reexport of Soviet oil and its derivatives. At present this second group of exports represents almost 10 percent of total exports. Ultimately this process has served to reduce the share of fuels, but at the same time there has been an increase in exports of electronic equipment and parts, pharmaceutical products and biotechnology (the export of vaccines has earned tens of millions of dollars since 1989), medical equipment, citrus and its processed by-products, textiles, and apparel (Figure 9.3).

The terms of trade of sugar improved markedly beginning in the 1970s with the establishment of price agreements with the member countries of the Council for Mutual Economic Assistance. Even though the terms of trade have fallen somewhat since 1980, their effect has remained favorable insofar as they have increased the overall share of sugar exports in any analysis based on the structure of exports at current prices. Studies which have recalculated the value of exports conclude that if export prices of 1965 were utilized, the share of sugar exports would amount to 75 percent of the total (Zimbalist and Brundenius, 1989).

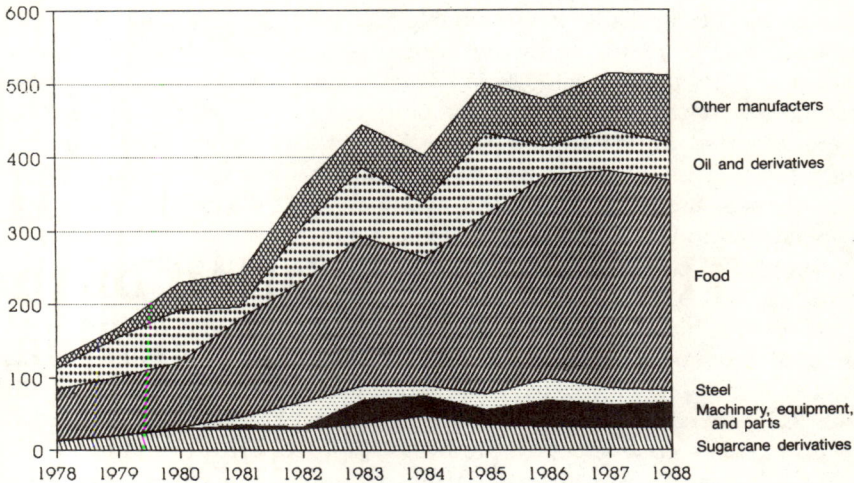

Figure 9.3   Performance of the second group of exports (millions of pesos), 1978-1988 (MINCEX, various years).

References

Castro, Fidel. 1959. *Fidel Castro: Conferencia de los delegados de las 21 repúblicas americanas*. Buenos Aires.

CEE (Comité Estatal de Estadísticas). 1987. *Anuario estadístico de Cuba*. Havana.

———. 1988. *Anuario estadístico de Cuba*. Havana.

———. n.d. *Desarrollo económica y social 1958-80*. Havana.

———. various years. *Anuario estadístico de Cuba*. Havana.

Foreign Policy Association. 1934. *Problemas de la nueva Cuba*. New York.

IBRD (International Bank for Reconstruction and Development). 1951. *Report on Cuba*. Washington, D.C.

MINCEX (Ministerio de Comercio Exterior). various years. *Resumen estadístico del comercio exterior*. Havana.

Ministerio de Hacienda. 1957. *Anuario Estadística de Cuba*. Havana.

Ministerio de Industrias. 1988. *CEE: Informe economía territorial*. Havana.

Wallich, Henry Christopher. 1951. *Problemas de una economía de exportación: La experiencia cubana de 1914-47*. Edited by the Banco Nacional de Cuba. Havana.

Zimbalist, Andrew, and Claes Brundenius. 1989. *The Cuban Economy: Measurement and Analysis of Socialist Performance*. Baltimore: Johns Hopkins University Press.

10

The Transformation of the Cuban Sugar Complex

Miguel Alejandro Figueras
Translated by Jennifer Dugan Abbassi

The production of sugar continues to be important in any analysis of the Cuban economy, but such analysis must reflect the qualitative changes that this traditionally stagnant subsector has undergone in the past thirty years.

Although sugarcane was cultivated as early as the seventeenth century, it was not until the beginning of the nineteenth century that the area devoted to it began to expand rapidly. This growth in sugar production was prompted by four events of the preceding century: the Industrial, the American, the French, and the Haitian revolutions. The number of sugar mills more than doubled, and in the second decade of the century technological advances in industrial equipment were introduced. Shortly thereafter, the railroad began to be used to carry the sugar to the ports.[1]

Because the first Cuban War of Independence (1868–1878) was fought primarily in the eastern part of the country, the resulting damage to sugar production was minor, for over 90 percent of sugarcane was cultivated in the west. At that time sugar mill owners were either *criollos* (Cuban-born of Spanish blood) or resident foreigners. At the end of the war, the number of sugar mills had been reduced by half, mainly through concentration. In the subsequent period (1880–1910), two developments proved decisive for the future: the emergence of monopolies in the United States with an interest in exporting capital to Latin American countries, of which Cuba was a high priority, and the sugar industry's construction of its own railroad to carry cane from the fields to the processing plants, thus making it feasible to replace the small mills with the large sugar factories originally called *centrales azucareros* (central sugar mills). It was at this point that the traditional agroindustrial link between ownership and management broke down, giving birth to the *colono* (planter) who sold his crop to a given sugar factory, either transporting it himself or using the factory's railroad, and establishing the technical and financial conditions for the birth of the large sugar estate. Even then, the penetration of foreign capital into Cuban sugar production remained moderate. In 1895, the second War of Independence broke out, but this time the situation was different: The war was fought in all parts of the country, and hundreds of sugar fields and processing plants were burned. On the eve of the war Cuba was producing more than 1 million tons of sugar a year. By the end of it production had been reduced to less than a third of that quantity. Although the British capital then dominant in Latin America was giving way to U.S. capital in Cuba, until 1910 the British still controlled half of the public railroads, a major share of the tobacco industry, the mining and banking sectors, and several sugar factories. U.S. capital took control of public services, built the other half of the public railroad system, established banking subsidiaries, and began to purchase land and sugar factories.

At the outset of World War I there was a balance between the overall capital invested in Cuba by British and by American corporations. The second decade of the century began with the opening of a large number of banking offices whose headquarters were located on the east coast of the United States, the simultaneous construction of dozens of large-scale sugar factories, mainly in Camagüey and Oriente provinces, and further acquisition of land and sugar factories by U.S. companies. These factors led to rapid growth in sugar production during the fifteen years between 1910 and 1925 from just under 2 million to over 6 million tons.

Two events of that period consolidated U.S. control over the Cuban economy and its sugar sector. The high price of sugar in the final phase of the war and immediately afterward triggered intense speculation that dragged down the Spanish and Cuban banks and, to a lesser extent, the banks of other countries. The collapse of sugar prices in 1920 was followed by the failure in October of that year of almost all the Spanish banks and a substantial number of Cuban ones. Because this bankruptcy affected most Cuban landowners, a significant portion of the sugar lands and industry became the property of U.S. banks and corporations. By that time, the international sugar market was in chronic crisis.

The crisis of 1920 combined with the effects of the Great Depression ten years later to produce a decline in the standard of living and income levels in Cuba. The mid-1920s saw the beginning of a phase of stagnation in Cuban sugar production, and in 1924 laws were passed restricting production to increase market prices. The Chadbourne Plan and later concessions had the effect of stimulating the production of crops other than sugar. From that point on, factories restricted themselves to the essential task of maintaining the fields for the next harvest (whose export quotas were established beforehand); technological innovation and cost reduction were postponed. The sugar sector stagnated and was decapitalized as funds were reoriented to other sectors or left the country. After 1925 not a single sugar factory was built, cultivation continued with the same structure of sugarcane varieties, and the railroad and other facilities were left to deteriorate. Fertilizer was used only in limited quantities. All of this took place while other sugar-producing countries were modernizing their agrotechnology and increasing their yield at a rate of 1.5 to 3.0 tons of cane per hectare per year. In Cuba, the average growth in a similar period was 300 kilograms per hectare per year. The following three decades were characterized by serious fluctuations, with many retreats and only very small advances, in Cuban sugar production. Although sugar continued to be the country's most important economic sector, its workers were employed only a few months out of the year, and their standard of living—particularly in the rural areas—was very low.

Changes Since the Revolution

As part of the revolution's socioeconomic program, the sugar sector was subjected to major changes. Improvement in the living and working conditions of the sugar workers and mechanization of sugar production were among the new government's top priorities. Part of the overall social investment was earmarked for improving the *bateyes* (villages) where many of these workers lived. More than fifteen thousand university graduates and several times this number of middle-level technicians, many of whom were the offspring of traditional sugar workers, were trained and incorporated into this sector. In addition to the human resources made available, the sugar sector has also received more than 9 billion Cuban pesos in productive investments over the past thirty years, accounting for 14–15 percent of the overall investments (productive and nonproductive) made by the state during this period.

During the first decade after the revolution the sugar sector received one-fifth of total investment. Although its share has decreased in recent years, it continues to be one of the top recipients. Part of this investment was directed at increasing production and improving working conditions, but for years a substantial portion of it was devoted to replacing outdated and fully depreciated equipment. Despite the effort to replace thousands of pieces of important machinery, 40 percent of the tandem mills, half of the boilers, and one-third of the turbogenerators are still in operation.

With a view to the expansion of productive capacity, the milling capacity of the 148 existing sugar factories has been increased to 82,000 tons a day, and 8 new sugar factories have been constructed over the last ten years with the capacity to produce 60,000 tons a day. The sugar intended for export is handled by seven specialized bulk terminals, which account for the shipping of 80 percent of the export produce.

The most important changes, however, relate to advances in agricultural production. The sugarcane varieties now under cultivation are different from those planted three decades ago. All land preparation is done mechanically with tractors, and 70 percent of the yield is harvested with combines. Three-quarters of the plantations use herbicides, resulting in a total use of 1 million tons of fertilizer compared with the 150,000–200,000-ton average for the 1950s. Approximately 30 percent of the cultivated area is or will soon be under irrigation.

The technical transformation of the backward sugar sector necessitated the establishment of an appropriate infrastructure, including mechanical workshops, warehouses, dams, and irrigation systems. Before 1959, 85–90 percent of the sugarcane was carried from the fields in oxcarts; at present, 99 percent is loaded into carts, tractors, or trucks, and this has required the construction of a substantial number of roads and byroads. Six thousand of the twelve thousand kilometers of railroad track existing in 1958 have been scrapped, and twenty-five hundred kilometers of additional track have been laid. Much of the rolling stock has been replaced, and the number of diesel locomotives has tripled in the past thirty years.

The total area under sugar cultivation has increased from 1.4–1.5 million hectares to 1.8 million hectares. However, while the yield has increased 25–30 percent, it is nonetheless below expectations based on the resources allocated to this crop in past years. Although technical and administrative factors have influenced this performance, it must be noted that the 1980s were one of the driest decades of the century, the first eight years of it having experienced only 16 percent of the average rainfall of the previous two decades. Cuba's tropical climate typically includes a cycle of four to five years of abundant rain during the appropriate season followed by a period of the same duration of relatively little rain. Even considering this pattern, however, the dry years of the 1980s are abnormal. The average annual rainfall between 1980 and 1988 was only 1,160 millimeters compared with an average of 1,350 millimeters for the two previous decades. From the yields over the past thirty years (Figure 10.1) it is apparent that *it is possible to increase yields in a short time*. The increasing use of irrigation involving divided drainage and efficient administration of these lands, along with advances in agrotechnology, may be expected to have this effect. All of this suggests that sugar production

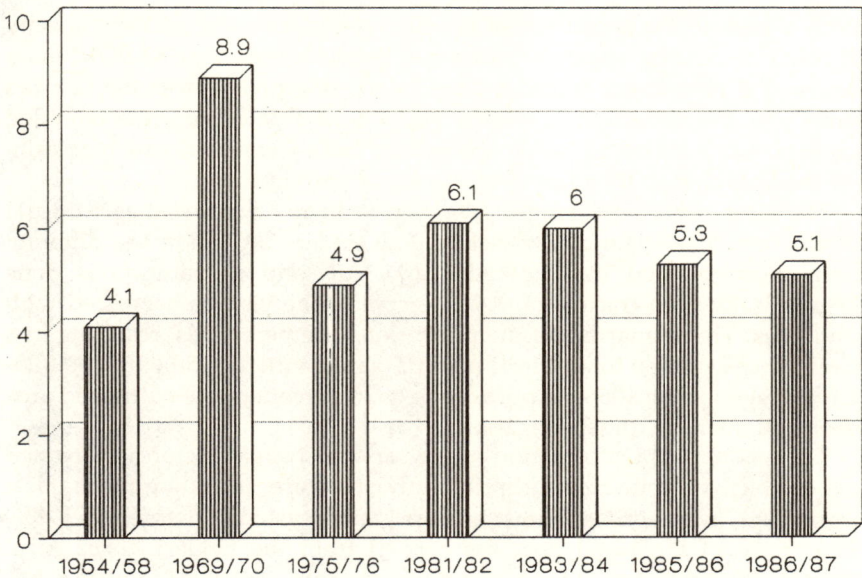

Figure 10.1   Sugarcane yields (tons per harvested hectare), 1954–1987 (CEE, various years).

in the 1980s will exceed 75 million tons, 38 percent more than the 56 million tons produced in the decade immediately preceding the revolution (Figure 10.2).

Over the past twenty-five years several Cuban research centers have undertaken studies of the possible utilization of sugarcane by-products as a source of raw materials for industrial purposes and for the production of food for human consumption and as feed for animals. With the exception of facilities producing alcohol and rum from molasses through a centuries-old process and small units producing artificial wood and paper from bagasse, however, an industry devoted to sugarcane derivatives has not yet been developed. The by-products that have been produced have nevertheless played an important role in the national economy. Of the fifty pulp and paper mills in operation worldwide, four are in Cuba, as are seven of the world's thirty-seven plants producing boards from bagasse. Other operations include ten torula yeast plants, seventeen alcohol distilleries, and several dozen rum factories, in addition to hundreds of units producing animal feeds. One of the most promising advances currently under trial is the production of saccharine, obtainable from sugarcane itself or from bagasse. Through a simple fermentation process it is possible to convert these inputs into a completely natural feed high

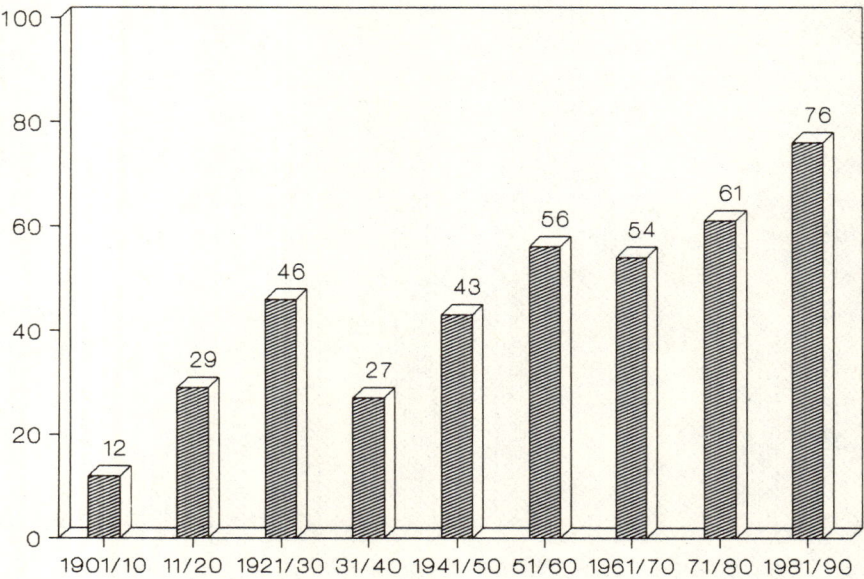

Figure 10.2   Twentieth-century sugarcane production (millions of tons) (CEE, various years).

in calories, proteins, and other nutrients, a natural resource for the feeding of cattle, swine, and poultry.

The dry years of the 1980s have seen notable achievements in the integration of sugar production and animal husbandry. The supply of feed to cattle during harvest seasons (when rainfall is scant and forage availability meager) has improved markedly. Some researchers have estimated that in recent years the sugar production complex has accounted for one-third of the overall feed requirements of the cattle population in dry seasons. Had it not been for the organized and massive use of sugarcane by-products and cane processing for animal feed, the performance of the cattle industry would have been disastrous in the extremely dry periods of 1986 and 1987, and several hundred thousand head of cattle would have died.

The production of sugarcane by-products (including the collection and processing of harvesting wastes) has come to account for an important share of the macroeconomic aggregates of the Cuban economy. The value of this production and its capital investment stands at approximately 3–4 percent of the corresponding industrial sector. In addition to such traditional export items as alcohol and rum, in recent years the scope of exports has widened to include torula yeast, paper, and simulated wood. The discovery of uses for sugarcane derivatives and the industrial processing of cane into animal feed are significant not only for Cuba but for all tropical countries that cultivate cane and are short of animal feed.

The industry that processes cane derivatives is now moving to so-called fourth-generation derivatives through biotechnology. By-products and derivatives of sugar are being used to produce phytosteroids, amino acids, cell grafts, and support for still enzymes, among other things (GEPLACEA, 1988).

Conclusion

Although other industries have grown at higher rates in recent years, sugar production continues to account for an important share of the economy. The productivity of this subsector influences not only the overall macroeconomic indicators but also the direct or indirect relations it has with other sectors; for example, a substantial part of animal-feeding capacity depends on sugarcane by-products. The land devoted to sugarcane production by agricultural enterprises, cooperatives, and farmers accounts for almost 1.9 million hectares, 46 percent of the total cultivated area. The rate of employment—both within and outside the state—in this subsector, including the by-product industries, represents 12 percent of total civil employment. Exports of sugar and its derivatives represent 75 percent of the total, translating into more than 400 pesos per capita of annual exports. Finally, sugar production accounts for 18 percent of the country's total capital investment and consumes one-third of the available energy. In 1957 the sugar subsector was estimated to have contributed 30 percent of the national income at factor cost. Although under the system of macroaggregates used in Cuba today the role of sugar in the economy is less than this (representing 11 percent of GSP), it is important not to underestimate its importance.

Notes

1. Sugar production in Cuba increased from 30,000 tons in 1810 to 90,000 by 1830, and from 220,000 in 1850 to 706,000 by 1985 (Guerra, 1920).

References

CEE (Comité Estatal de Estadísticas). various years. *Anuario Azucarero de Cuba.* Havana.

GEPLACEA (Group of Latin American and Caribbean Sugar-Exporting Countries). 1988. *Manual de los derivados de la caña de azúcar.* N.p.: United Nations Program for Development.

Guerra, Ramiro. 1920. *Azúcar y población de las Antillas.* Havana: Ciencias Sociales.

PART 3
Social Questions

11
Youth and the Cuban Revolution

Juan Luis Martín
Translated by Aníbal Yáñez

For the past thirty years Cuban youth has experienced uninterrupted upward social mobility. This trend is apparent in the increase in the level of schooling with decreasing age: while in the fifty-five to fifty-nine-year age-group the level of technical-professional schooling and higher education is 8.06 percent, in the thirty-five to thirty-nine-year age-group it is 14.89 percent and in the twenty-five to twenty-nine-year age-group as high as 17.64 percent (CEE, 1981:169–170, Table 40). The age-group composition of the occupational structure also shows this upward mobility: 42.8 percent of the country's professionals and technicians are between seventeen and twenty-nine years of age (CEE, 1985). Similarly, 62.8 percent of rural youth are incorporated into advanced forms of organization of labor such as production cooperatives (CEE, 1986:113–114, Table 4). In key branches of the economy such as electronics, the machine tool industry, and mining and metallurgy, young workers make up more than 40 percent of the total work force (CEE, 1985).

These indicators are the result of a policy, maintained throughout the history of the revolution, of giving priority to mass education and guaranteeing access to it to young people of all social sectors. Within this general framework, a historical approach to the issue allows an appreciation of changes in the role of Cuban youth with regard to society as a whole—changes shaped both by the transformations in the country's economic and social situation and by the age-group's internal dynamics.

During the 1960s and the first half of the 1970s these transformations and internal changes took place with unprecedented speed. The resources obtained through the expropriation first of foreign enterprises and later of the national bourgeoisie, together with aid from the socialist camp, allowed for accelerated growth of investment that generated a significant increase and diversification in employment. The rate of investment rose to more than 30 percent of the gross social product. The impact of this process on employment can be appreciated by comparing the 59 types of technical occupations existing in 1953 with the 118 existing in 1981 (CETSS, 1981:204–205, Table 54 and Resolution 654). The socialist character of the revolution guaranteed a redistribution of income that was expressed in vast education and health programs providing unprecedented opportunities to the entire population. The revolutionary transformation of property relations generated a reaction in the form of the emigration of members of social classes that had been owners of the means of production and people imbued with the values of these classes who saw their expectations of consumption or accumulation blocked by the new model of society. The conjunction of these factors opened up a broad social and economic space for the youth of the 1960s.

The establishment of the foundations for the new social order under constant attack by imperialism and internal counterrevolution left a deep mark on the process of socialization of the young, who from the outset were in the vanguard in the great tasks of the day: literacy campaigns, defense, sugar and coffee harvests, construction of public works, and so on. From their ranks came the officers and cadres of the armed forces, the new intellectuals who replaced those who had left for the United States, and the skilled labor for the many new enterprises. The socialization process that took shape under these conditions drew its dynamic from the leaders' great confidence in youth, and it resulted in the internationalization of a set of social values in tune with the goals of the revolution that made that generation a solid base of support for the building of socialism. These same factors had a somewhat different impact upon the children of this period, who today constitute the largest proportion of the population.

The end of the war of liberation and the aforementioned social transformations produced a demographic boom, with birth rates that reached 35 percent between 1959 and 1964 and remained over 29 percent until 1972 (CEE, 1985:30–34). After that date there was a sharp decrease that has continued to this day, the result of the spread of the use of birth control, the increase in the level of education, and an increase in social activity. This process has produced a bulge in the age pyramid that has certain social and economic implications. For one thing, because the proportion of youth in the population has risen to 33.23 percent (and to

45.41 percent of the population of working age) youth now constitute the largest age-group in the population (CEE, 1987:58, Table 11.2). At the same time, the reduction in the birth rate since 1972 means that the group born between 1959 and 1964 is predominant within youth as a whole and sets the tone for the age-group's interests and expectations. This group's entry into the stage of "early youth" (fourteen to seventeen years) between 1973 and 1981 shaped a social image of young people as students and tended to focus the attention of youth organizations and of society as a whole upon students' problems. Its transition to "middle youth" (eighteen to twenty-four years) between 1977 and 1988 produced an increase in attention to the problems of young workers. Its arrival at "mature youth" (twenty-five to thirty years) between 1984 and 1994 made this subgroup predominant, a situation that will continue throughout the 1990s. The shift in focus to problems related to employment and work was clearly expressed in the Unión de Jóvenes Comunistas, where for the first time since the triumph of the revolution topics having to do with young workers were analyzed more extensively than problems of students. This trend will probably continue through the sixth and seventh congresses. Indeed, the process has been characterized by a gradual "graying" of youth, who have evolved from being an eminently student group to one made up predominantly of workers, laborers, and intellectual workers making up 46 percent of all youth (CEE, 1986:92–93, Table 2).

As the generation of the demographic boom has gradually risen in the age pyramid, the entry of successive cohorts had an impact upon various social subsystems. An avalanche of entries into the educational system's elementary level forced rapid growth at that level. Society was faced with the choice of either increasing its educational capacities at breakneck speed—even if this meant slower development in the qualitative sense— or allowing part of a generation to go without education. The moral imperative of guaranteeing education to all citizens, along with the need to help other Third World countries in technical fields and to maintain a reservoir of skilled labor sufficient in size to survive in the event of war and undertake the reconstruction of the country, led to the decision to spare no effort in broadening the educational system. This goal was fully met, and educational opportunities for enormous numbers of children and youth were ensured.

When this group began to reach working age after 1976, the demand for employment and housing increased accordingly, and it is projected to reach a peak between 1989 and 1991 (CEE, 1988). This trend coincides with a period of difficulties resulting, on the one hand, from errors in economic policy and other spheres of social life, the rectification of which has been one of the revolution's fundamental objectives since 1986 and, on the other, from the constant worsening of the international economic situation for the Third World. Although Cuba is part of the socialist community, its development has been adversely affected by the openness of its economy and the necessary exchange of part of its production with capitalist countries—not to mention the ever-present effects of the thirty-year-long economic blockade imposed by the United States, which requires some trade routes to be fourteen thousand miles long instead of ninety. Just as in the 1960s the massive entry of school-age children was a challenge to the creativity and vision of the revolution, addressed by the combination of unity and flexibility of which a socialist society with a planned economy is capable, in the 1980s and 1990s the problem of generating and distributing employment has been one of the main issues.

There are a number of barriers to the entry of youth into employment. Some of these, such as the seniority system, have a tradition and roots in the working class; others, such as "job qualifiers" (norms that set the requirements for entry to one or another occupation), are widespread in society. These issues were analyzed by the youth themselves during the fifth congress of the UJC and resulted in discussions with the institutions involved, from the trade unions to the state work committee, that led to modifications in organizational norms. Other formulas that offer solutions to the problem are differential generation of employment according to the territory's labor supply through increased investment in that territory and the choice of high-, medium-, or low-intensity technology in order to match production requirements with the employment rate to be generated. The concepts about building socialism that shape the problem-solving process play an important role in the identification and implementation of these solutions. To have maintained a conception of the socialist economy based upon monetary commodity relations would have made it difficult to avoid generational competition for jobs and thus distorted the cooperative and complementary intergenerational relations that should prevail in socialism by creating a false image of conflicting interests. Generations do exist in socialism, with distinctive features dictated by the concrete historical conditions under which their needs, interests, and expectations have developed. Differences and even partial and conjunctural contradictions may arise among them, but these will not be antagonistic because their particular interests are contained within the larger historical interests of the social classes to which they belong.

The issue of employment among youth has a conjunctural character that will be overcome within the next five years at the most. The truly strategic objective of the coming years will be the development of a social consciousness with an important ethical component, one of its main features being love of work. The youth of the 1990s will be predominantly mature, for the most part laborers and intellectual workers, with a high level of schooling, a high degree of information due to the density of the mass media network, and the expectations of a high degree of social interaction both because of the life-style created by socialist society and because of the rapid increase in urbanization. This youth will play the leading role in society by about 2005, in a world probably characterized by a deepening of the contradictions between developed and underdeveloped countries and an ongoing scientific-technical revolution that will increase the social and international division of labor, bringing with it rapid change in spheres ranging from art and culture to leadership. This period will probably coincide with the physical extinction of the generation that initiated and propelled the revolution and will undoubtedly be a moment when the social system's capacity for stable development will be put to the test. The task of the Cuban Revolution remains to strengthen and develop the economy, the system of institutions, law, and democracy and to form a citizenry with a strong sense of social responsibility. The achievement of this goal will entail constant improvement of the socialization process, increasing its systematic character and thus the relations of complementarity among its basic institutions: family, school, social organizations, labor institutions, mass media, cultural and sports institutions, and the judicial system. It will also entail the active participation of youth in the construction and leadership of the society and a capacity on the part of the socializing institutions for change in objectives and methods with changes in social reality. These are the tasks that are being undertaken, and a number of experiments are now taking place.

Efforts are being made to increase the participation of worker collectives and of local leaders in the management of their firms and establishments. The scope of university courses and of training in technical schools is being increased by the development of broader programs that can adapt to the changing conditions of production. Educational experiments are being directed at developing the role of youth in education and the importance of moral education within education as a whole, while other projects aim to accelerate and improve the process of assimilating university graduates into production. The role of the community in the planning and control of cultural and recreational work and the democratic nature of this process are being developed. All of these tasks have as a common starting point the principle that inspires the rectification process now under way in the Cuban Revolution: confidence in human beings and their ability to find solutions to problems, no matter how difficult, once convinced of the rationale for and the necessity of their work.

References

CEE (Comité Estatal de Estadísticas). 1981. *Censo de población y viviendas.* Vol. 16. Havana.

———— . 1985. *Modelos de trabajo y salarios: Modelo 7609.* Havana.

———— . 1986. *Encuesta nacional de ocupación, 1985.* Havana.

———— . 1987. *Anuario Estadístico de Cuba.* Havana.

———— . 1988. "Programa de investigaciones sobre la juventud," in *Proyección de la población joven de Cuba, 1987–2005.* Havana.

CETSS (Comité Estatal de Trabajo y Seguridad Social). 1981. *Censo de población, viviendas y electoral, 1953.* Havana.

12

Social Policy and the Family in Socialist Cuba

Inés Cristina Reca
Translated by Sarah Stookey

The social contributions of the family cannot be understood outside the larger context of the society and, specifically, without reference to the mode of production. Socialist relations of production form an objective foundation for family relations based on mutual attraction, love, and respect between man and woman and shared responsibility for the care and education of children. The socialist family does not, however, arise automatically or without contradictions, nor does it develop with the same vigor or at the same rate across all classes and social groups. In every socialist society historical processes, the relations of production, the structure of classes, and the character of the political and ideological struggle determine the various factors—living conditions, values, traditions, and cultural levels—that influence the development of the family. In Cuba, transformations brought about by the revolution—among them the elimination of unemployment, the redistribution of income, agrarian reform, the incorporation of women into the work force, universal primary education and increased opportunities for technical and professional development for adults, access to health care and special mother/infant programs, and so forth—have dramatically influenced the characteristics and functions of the Cuban family today.[1]

In the 1970s, the period of institutionalization of revolutionary gains, many changes were written into law. The family was defined as "an entity in which social and personal interests are intimately related" and as "the center of the life shared by women and men, parents and children and family members in general, satisfying deep human, emotional and social interests" (Código de familia, 1980:6). Article 34 of the 1976 constitution established the state's obligation to protect the family, maternity, and marriage, and Article 35 specified that the protection of marriage was based on "the absolute equality of obligations and rights of the couple to contribute to the maintenance of the home and the holistic development of children in a manner that is compatible with the social activities of each individual." The rights of children, whatever their paternity, were also established. Articles 26 and 27 regulated conjugal relationships and dictated shared responsibility for the care of the family, the education and guidance of children, and the satisfaction of family needs, each according to his/her abilities and economic capacity. "If one is primarily responsible for the housework and the care of children, the other partner should be primarily responsible for the necessary subsistence, without infringing on their obligation to cooperate in domestic work" (Article 27). The family code further regulates marriage, divorce, parent-child relationships, and obligations for the provision of basic needs and support. It was widely discussed at the grass-roots level by the Comités de Defensa de la Revolución, the Central de Trabajadores de Cuba, the Federación de Mujeres Cubanas, and other mass organizations.

Naturally, the legal formulation of these principles did not guarantee an immediate change in the traditional division of domestic labor between the sexes. In Cuba as in other Latin American countries, patriarchal domination influenced by the Hispanic-Christian tradition and African culture has left its imprint on social values and norms. Appeals to their "historic," "natural," or "biological" roles have charged women with the responsibility of domestic work and child care, generally subordinating them and restricting their opportunities for participation in other spheres of social activity. Although these beliefs are frequently identified with the term *machismo*, some women share responsibility for their transmission to their sons and daughters.

Change in the Cuban family has generally been positive, but problematic patterns of family relations persist. These derive in large part from the contradictions that arise as women are incorporated into economic activity and as efforts are made to achieve equality for women in all areas of national life. Cuban social policies that have influenced the development of the family include those dealing with demographics, women's participation in the work force, education, health, and housing.

Population Policies

Among the population policies that have affected the family, those concerned with the evolution of the fertility rate, the rate at which new families are formed, and family size are of particular interest.

The general objective of population policy has been the creation of more favorable conditions for population growth, including a lower rate of morbidity and progressive improvements in living conditions, life expectancy, and the distribution through the national health system of the means and services necessary for voluntary birth control. Since 1959 the Cuban population has experienced moderate growth (9.2 per 1,000 for 1981–1986), a low birth rate (16.3 per 1,000), low general infant mortality (6.2 deaths per 1,000 live births), and high life expectancy (74.2 years) (all figures for 1986; CEE, 1986:73, 78).These levels, especially for infant mortality, are characteristic of developed countries and represent one of Cuba's most significant achievements.

In the late 1950s, Cuba showed a net population growth of 20.2 per 1,000, with a gross birth rate of 27.3 per 1,000, a mortality rate of 6.4 per 1,000, and a negative migration rate of −0.7 per 1,000 (Farnós, 1979:126). In the first years after 1959 there was a dramatic increase (2.2 percent) in the growth rate, and demographics began to reflect the impact of revolutionary policies. Between 1959 and 1963 the overall fertility rate[2] increased from 3.7 to 4.7 per woman of childbearing age. This shift is usually attributed to greater job security, the redistribution of income, and better health and education opportunities as well as the increase in marriages, shortage of birth-control products due to the U.S. blockade, and restrictions on abortions. The impact of these factors was temporary, however, and by the end of the 1960s growth rates had returned to their previous levels: In 1970 the overall fertility rate was again 3.7 (Catasús et al., 1987:Table 8, #5).

Beginning in 1971, the overall birth rate fell rapidly from 29.5 to its lowest level, 15.0, in 1981. This change was reflected in a reduction in the average size of the family from 4.9 persons in 1953 to 4.1 in 1981. Today the population continues to grow slowly, despite the fact that between 1981 and 1985 the annual growth rate showed an increase from 6.2 to 10.8 per thousand as the population born during the immediate postrevolutionary period began to reproduce. In 1986 the annual growth rate of the population reached 9.1.

In reviewing these demographic changes two important trends emerge. First, the significant and rapid decrease in the fertility rate led to negative population growth between 1979 and 1984, the last year for which full data are available (Table 12.1). The prospect of sustained negative growth has prompted some specialists to recommend that couples be encouraged to have at least two or three children (Farnós, 1985). Second, the Cuban population is aging. The 1970 census showed a total population of 8.6 million, with 36.9 percent under fourteen years of age and 9.0 percent sixty years of age or older. In 1981, of a total population of 9.7 million,

TABLE 12.1   Gross Birth Rates and Gross Reproduction Rates (daughters per woman), 1970–1986

Year	Gross Birth Rate	Gross Reproduction Rate
1970	27.5	1.80
1971	29.5	1.88
1972	28.1	1.80
1973	25.1	1.61
1974	22.2	1.42
1975	20.8	1.33
1976	19.9	1.27
1977	17.7	1.12
1978	15.4	0.94
1979	14.8	0.88
1980	14.1	0.81
1981	14.0	0.78
1982	16.3	0.89
1983	16.7	0.90
1984	16.6	0.88
1985	18.0	—
1986	16.3	—

Sources: CEE (1986:73), Catasús et al. (1987: Table 8, #40).

these groups amounted to 30.3 percent and 10.8 percent of the population, respectively.

Women in the Work Force

An intense and sustained incorporation of women into the work force is linked to both decreases in the size of the family and changes in the configuration of family roles. In the first years after the start of the revolution, the FMC developed diverse education, training, and political consciousness programs for women. Although the pressing need for trained labor was instrumental, the incorporation of women into the work force was not simply a matter of necessity. Rather, it formed a basic component of policies aimed at the full integration of women into society. One of the fundamental values of the revolution has been that human beings can realize their full potential only through creative and productive work. A woman's independent involvement in economic labor encourages her personal development, allows her to become better informed, and increases her opportunities for participation in union and political activity. Clearly, it is impossible to struggle for the creation of a new society and the transformation of consciousness without struggling for the complete integration and liberation of women. From the very beginning this issue has been emphasized by the revolutionary leadership: It was presented in the 1975 document "On the Full Exercise of Women's Equality" and in four congresses of the FMC.

The unstable and subordinate position of women in the work force before 1959 made them economically dependent on men, first as fathers and then as husbands. According to the 1953 census, one in seven women worked outside the home, "solely out of [economic] need." Women made up only 13.7 percent of the work force (256,440) and were concentrated in jobs with low qualifications. Only 16.2 percent of working women were in the professional and technical fields, and of this group 83.8 percent were elementary-school teachers. The principal industrial sectors open to women were tobacco and textiles, of which they made up 35 percent and 46 percent of the work force, respectively. More than a third of working women were domestic employees (27.2 percent) and chambermaids (3.9 percent). Only 8 percent of all women had received a primary education, 3 percent a secondary education, and a mere 0.6 percent a university degree. More than one in five women were illiterate (Colectivo de autores, 1987).

The increase in female employment between 1960 and 1980 averaged 8 percent annually, surpassing by a wide margin the increase in male employment. By 1985 there were 1,200,000 women in the work force, representing 37.2 percent of the total and 43.3 percent of all women of working age. It is significant that advances similar to those that cost European and North American women a century of struggle have been achieved by Cuban women in little more than twenty years.

In addition to these dramatic quantitative gains, there has been improvement in the forms of women's participation. Women participate today in all kinds of work, including that in the areas of greatest scientific and technical progress. Data from the census of 1981 show that 33.3 percent of the economically active population were engaged in intellectual work, of which 51 percent was performed by women. Within this general category women made up 29.8 percent of workers in the field of engineering and technology, 61.7 percent of workers in teaching and scientific research, 72.8 percent of workers in medicine, and 37.7 percent of workers in the planning and administration of the national economy (CEE, 1981:ccxii). In 1985 52.9 percent of all technicians and professionals were women, most of whom were concentrated in the categories of administrative and service personnel, making up 83.1 percent and 63.9 percent of these, respectively.

An analysis of the marital status of working women shows that in 1970 29.9 percent of single women (fifteen years and older) and 47.6 percent of divorced women were active in the work force. These figures were much higher than the 13.9 percent for women in conjugal relationships. In this Cuba did not differ from other Latin American countries; despite

TABLE 12.2   Percentage of Female Participation in the Work Force and Fertility Rate by Age-Group, 1953, 1970, and 1981

Age-Group	Work-Force Participation			Fertility Rate		
	1953	1970	1981	1953	1970	1981
15–19	17.25	16.41	12.88	58.9	128.5	81.2
20–24	22.27	25.26	43.22	205.6	229.0	111.5
25–29	22.12	24.17	50.87	203.6	164.6	68.8
30–34	21.26	23.03	52.37	138.8	114.2	36.6
35–39	21.14	22.18	51.76	79.1	74.0	14.7
40–44	20.90	21.09	48.68	28.7	26.4	4.2
45–49	19.58	18.91	40.70	4.2	4.9	0.6

Source: González (1986: Tables II.4 and II.7).

TABLE 12.3   Women's Participation in Executive Positions, 1974 and 1984

	PCC		UJC		CDR		ANAP	
	1974	1984	1974	1984	1974	1984	1974	1984
Municipal	2.9	18.9	22.0	32.1	7.0	37.5	16.3	18.0
Provincial	6.3	16.9	7.0	28.9	3.0	37.5	1.1	16.0
National	5.5	12.8	10.0	27.1	19.0	31.8	2.0	11.0

Source: Espín (1986: 55).

the measures implemented, conceptions about women's economic role in the family had not changed. By 1981 this situation had changed significantly. One in every three women in conjugal relationships was active in the labor force; the participation of single women was 35.4 percent and of divorced and separated women 53.8 percent. Increases in the rates of work-force participation between 1970 and 1980 are closely associated with decreases in the reproductive level of different age-groups, with the exception of fifteen- to nineteen-year-olds. This helps to explain the decrease in reproduction among women over thirty (Table 12.2).

Women's participation in leadership roles in political, labor, and mass organizations is strongest at the grass-roots level. Between 1974 and 1984, an increasing number of women were promoted within the Partido Comunista de Cuba, but underrepresentation in the leadership at the municipal and national levels persists (Table 12.3). In 1984 women accounted for only 33.9 percent and 21.4 percent of the delegates in the National Assembly and Poder Popular, respectively. Analogous tendencies are evident in the participation of women in leadership roles in the central administration of the state; the figures are relatively low considering women's participation in the work force. For example, 10.9 percent of directors and 12.6 percent of subdirectors are women. In the health sector, in which 68.9 percent of the workers are women, they represent only 39 percent of the directors (Espín, 1986:49–50). Within the labor movement,

TABLE 12.4   Average Time (hours:minutes) Dedicated to Domestic Tasks, 1979 and 1985

	Working Men		Working Women		Nonworking Women		Students	
	1979	1985	1979	1985	1979	1985	1979	1985
Workday	1:03	1:35	3:54	2:47	7:81	7:46	1:16	0:39
Nonworkday	1:31	1:22	5:45	5:46	7:27	6:22	0:58	1:17

Sources: INSIE (1979), CEE (1986).

data from 1983 show that at the level of union sections 45.1 percent of the delegates were women in comparison with 14.7 percent in provincial committees and the professional cadre of the national leadership.

Analysis of this issue by the Party and the FMC suggests that the obstacles to women's integration into leadership structures are both objective and subjective. The objective ones include the limitations inherent in the development of the productive forces, the organization of work, the shortage of domestic help and time-saving equipment, and the lack of child care facilities. Among the subjective ones are the conception of women as solely responsible for domestic chores and child rearing and the overburdening that this produces ("the double shift"), the preference given to men in workplace promotions, ideas about "protecting" women that limit their access to various kinds of work, persistent traditions that reflect a double standard in sexual relations, and women's assimilation as "natural" or beliefs that encourage them to remain in traditional social roles or make the obstacles to greater political and social responsibility seem insurmountable.

As we have seen, the establishment of legal norms regulating shared responsibilities and social activity in general have not transformed the traditional sexual division of work. Although changes have occurred in some groups, they have not become general (Table 12.4). Participation in the work force tends to lengthen women's workdays because they continue to be responsible for the majority of household chores. Generally, between 1979 and 1985 all of the groups studied showed reductions in the average amount of time spent daily on domestic tasks, but women continue to be primarily responsible for this work. Both working women and housewives spent less time on domestic tasks, 2.47 hours and 7.46 hours in 1985 instead of 3.54 and 7.51 hours in 1979, respectively. Whereas the reduction of time spent for housewives is greater on weekends than on weekdays, working women postpone much of this work to the weekend, when they dedicate an average of 5.46 hours to it. This use of their "nonworking" time implies a corresponding reduction of their free time. The results of a 1984 national study of the free time of youth (in the fourteen- to thirty-year age-group) also showed significant differences between men and

TABLE 12.5   Average Time (hours:minutes) Spent by Youth on Domestic Tasks, 1984

	Urban Students		Rural Students		Urban Workers		Rural Workers	
	Female	Male	Female	Male	Female	Male	Female	Male
Workday	0:46	0:08	0:52	0:13	1:36	0:27	2:50	0:16
Nonworkday	1:12	0:20	0:55	0:04	3:32	1:21	4:15	0:38

Source: Fernández et al. (1987: Table 4, #71).

women in the time invested in domestic tasks and demonstrates that for Cuban youth these tasks continue to be typically feminine activities (Table 12.5). More study is necessary to determine whether the little time spent by male youths on these tasks should be understood as indicating the persistence of traditional values or a tendency to overprotect the younger generation by exempting them from household responsibilities. More than anything expressed verbally, this pattern of sexual division of domestic work, reinforced daily, establishes masculine and feminine behaviors that do not encourage the development of socialist family relations.

> It is necessary for both men and women to become conscious of this behavior, since by the weight of custom many women make themselves solely responsible for domestic tasks and, when they talk about involving their husbands or sons, propose that they "help." Similarly, many men assert proudly that they regularly "help" their wives. What we really need is for everyone to consider domestic work a family responsibility to be shared. (Espín, 1986:49–50)

Education and Health Policies

Since its first days, the Cuban Revolution has devoted its greatest efforts to health and education. The 1953 census showed very low levels of education, with illiteracy rates of 23.6 percent for the general population and 41.7 percent in rural areas. Current figures show a growing level of education and training for work and for political and social activity. Census data from 1981 show that only 2.7 percent of the children aged six to twelve were not attending school. Whereas in 1953 only 15 percent of all children had matriculated, 55 percent had in 1981. The volume of graduates from the various levels had increased fourfold by 1981. Enrollment in the institutes of advanced pedagogy in 1985–1986 reached 107,000, 77 percent more than the preceding five-year period.

That in 1981 more than half of the population of both sexes had finished at least elementary school meant that the Cuban couple of the 1980s had the potential for broader interests and cultural experiences and, consequently, enhanced family roles, but the persistence of lower educational levels for women has serious consequences for family life. Both national (Álvarez et al., 1987) and regional (Domínguez, 1986:83–86) studies have established a relationship between low education level and early reproduction (under twenty years). Teenage pregnancy and the use of abortion as a means of birth control are the object of study, and serious efforts are being made to develop the sexual awareness necessary for the establishment of a healthy relationship and, later, a healthy marriage and family.[3]

Health policies have been based on the principles of the responsibility of the state for guaranteeing this service, coordination and planning of services, and popular participation. The national health system ensures medical attention and especially prevention services and health education, mother/infant care, and family medicine. The newest of these health services, family medicine, was instituted three years ago. In this program a doctor and a nurse attend to 120 families, making house calls and offering preventive medicine and health education on the basis of a more in-depth understanding of the life-styles of their patients. This program has had a dramatic impact in isolated rural areas. One significant indicator of the level of attention is the increase in the proportion of doctors from 1 per 1,067 inhabitants in 1958 to 1 per 636 in 1980 and 1 per 443 in 1985.

The programs for pregnant women that have special relevance for a discussion of the family include prenatal visits, diagnosis, and attention to high-risk pregnancies as well as such relatively sophisticated programs as fertility consultations and the detection of congenital cardiac conditions using the most modern technology. Before 1959 the majority of births occurred outside of medical facilities. As a result of the expansion of the network of maternity hospitals, between 1970 and 1981 the percentage of live births increased from 91.5 to 98.8. Infant mortality (under 1 year of age) has undergone a significant reduction, reaching a level of 13.6 deaths per 1,000 live births.

Another aspect of social policy that favors the family is the legal, social, and economic protection afforded pregnant women. The law provides for fully paid leave for a period of time before and twelve weeks after the birth; job security is guaranteed for up to one year. Both in-patient and out-patient care and medicines are provided free of charge, and supplementary food is distributed. Furthermore, the national health system provides women with the information and means for voluntary birth control.

Of special importance for the care of young children are the day-care centers, supervised by educators and specialized personnel, where children receive, in addition to educational activities, medical attention and a nutritionally balanced diet (Table 12.6). Since day-care services are partially subsidized, they represent a form of income supplement. Whereas

TABLE 12.6   Number, Enrollment, and Personnel of Day-care Centers, 1977–1986

	1977	1978	1981	1983	1985	1986
Number	713	802	838	835	844	854
Enrollment	65,056	92,103	91,772	97,596	109,352	109,923
Children under five per 10,000 attending	500	874	1,004	1,127	1,117	1,170
Technical personnel	20,984	10,698	13,706	14,982	18,793	20,194

Source: CEE (1986a: 513, 514).

the cost of maintaining a child is 70–75 pesos monthly, parent contributions fluctuate between 5 and 40 pesos according to family income. Similarly, the school meal programs, secondary school, technical, and other kinds of subsidies also contribute to the value of family income.

As a result of these programs and services, the Cuban family can rely on comprehensive health and education benefits for its members and special attention for children.

The Housing Problem

Housing is a basic necessity that has a direct impact on the quality and feasibility of family life. The program approved by the third Party congress in 1985 defines the commitment to work so that "each family has comfortable housing . . . within the context of the possibilities of economic development" (PCC, 1987:44). Comparison of the conditions that existed before 1959 with the current housing situation reveals positive changes in the number of units constructed, accessibility and affordability, the quality of the materials used, and the availability of electricity and potable water.

In Fidel's *History Will Absolve Me* we find the following depiction of the housing situation before 1959: "There are in Cuba 200,000 shacks and huts, 400,000 families in the rural and urban areas live in shantytowns, 200,000 of our urban population pay rents that consume between a fifth and a third of their income, and 2,800,000 of our rural and suburban population lack electricity" (Castro, 1953:37–38). According to census figures for 1953, 33.3 percent of all housing units had walls made of leaves or palm fronds; 82.2 percent of these houses were in rural areas. Only 34 percent of all units had indoor plumbing; in the urban areas the figure was 52.6 percent and in the rural areas only 2.4 percent.

As a result of the policies implemented by the revolution, the population and housing census of 1981 shows that 47.1 percent of the houses and apartments in the country as a whole and 66.6 percent of the houses in the rural areas were built after 1959. Also according to the 1981 census,

49.7 percent of all units (68.9 percent of the urban and 9.2 percent in the rural areas) had indoor plumbing. Whereas in 1953 only 55.6 percent of all units and only 8.1 percent in the rural areas had electricity, in 1981 these figures were 88.9 percent and 47.7 percent, respectively (CEE, 1981).[4] This improvement has had a significant impact on family life, facilitating domestic work and making the house a place in which the family can enjoy its free time with television and radio.

The average number of inhabitants per dwelling has also been slowly reduced, from 4.8 in 1953 to 4.5 in 1970 and 4.1 in 1981. At the same time there has been an increase in the average size of dwellings; whereas in 1953 only 16.7 percent of the dwellings had more than four rooms, in 1984 this percentage had risen to 49.5 percent. These global indicators do not reflect population density in the provinces, urban centers, and municipalities. Furthermore, a large percentage of the houses in Old Havana are old and in a state of disrepair. In an attempt to address these problems, the process of rectification has since 1987 encouraged the formation of microbrigades to perform rehabilitation work. Despite these efforts, however, a serious housing deficit persists.

In addition to the construction of housing, there is a need for community infrastructure such as clinics, schools, day-care centers, stores, and markets. An example of the effectiveness of the new strategy is the construction by the microbrigades of 54 day-care centers with a capacity for 11,340 children in Havana in December 1987 and approximately double that number in 1988.

The distribution of household appliances is also important for the material quality of family life. More widespread access to electricity has been accompanied by increased ownership of consumer goods. As of 1984 the average numbers of various appliances per 100 dwellings were 117.1 stoves (including kerosene), 110.9 radios, 94.7 electric irons, 74.6 black-and-white televisions, 70.9 fans, and 64.9 refrigerators. For some important labor-saving machines, for example, refrigerators, washing machines (43.8 per 100), and coffee percolators (38.9 per 100), average ownership is still unsatisfactory. Finally, there are problems in both the quality and the availability of services such as laundromats and appliance and furniture repair shops.

The Cuban Family: A Synthesis

Even from this brief study, it is possible to make some basic generalizations about the Cuban family today. In the first place, the number of family units has grown at a rate slightly higher than the rate of growth of the population; in the period 1970–1981 the rate of population growth was 1.1 percent compared with 1.9 percent for family units. The average

TABLE 12.7   Private Census Nuclei and Population by Type of Nucleus

Type	Private Nuclei		Population	
	Thousands	*Percentage*	*Thousands*	*Percentage*
One-person	209.8	6.9	209.8	2.2
Basic[a]	1,262.8	53.7	4,790.7	49.4
Extended	763.6	32.5	4,053.4	41.9
Composite	114.8	4.9	627.2	6.5
Total	2,351.0	100.0	9,681.1	100.0

[a]Couple without children, couple with one or more children, mother or father with one or more children.

Source: CEE (1981: Table 68, cxxxvii).

TABLE 12.8   Family Units (percentage) by Composition, 1979

Composition	Urban	Rural	Total
Nuclear	56.9	66.8	60.3
Couple with children	38.9	53.0	43.8
Couple without children	9.1	8.3	8.7
Mother or father with children	8.9	5.5	7.8
Extended	43.1	33.2	39.7
Head, other relatives	12.9	10.2	11.9
Head, spouse, other relatives	2.7	2.2	2.5
Head, spouse, children, other relatives	18.0	16.4	17.5
Head, children, other relatives	9.5	4.4	7.8
Total	100.0	100.0	100.0

Source: CEE (n.d.: Table 24, 82–83).

size of the family has diminished, and so has the difference in family size between rural and urban areas. In 1981 the average family consisted of 4.1 persons, compared with 4.9 in 1953. This trend reflects the slow growth rate of the population and the decrease in reproductivity.

With respect to the different forms of family units, in 1981 the nuclear family predominated (53.7 percent of total units) over two- and three-generational families (32.5 percent of total units), but multigenerational families represented 41.9 percent of the total population (Table 12.7). The proportion of nuclear families is higher when the category is broadened to include residential families, as the demographic survey of 1979 permits (Table 12.8). Furthermore, the proportion of nuclear family units in rural areas is significantly higher than the national average. The greater proportion of these units in rural areas may be due to the greater availability of housing there. If this is the case, it might be assumed that in the urban centers, especially the larger ones, alongside the multigenerational families there are smaller extended families headed by women, perhaps formed in the aftermath of divorce.

Lack of housing, especially in the urban areas, has been considered one of the factors that inhibits the formation of nuclear families. Although figures on the rate of family formation exist only for 1979 and 1981, it is apparent that many young couples are forced to continue living with their parents, eventually forming three-generational families. The census data on family relations show an increase in the proportion of grandchildren living with heads of families: 4.3 percent in 1953, 5.0 percent in 1970, and 7 percent in 1981. The high proportion of extended families in the urban areas seems to be more the result of limitations in housing than of cultural patterns. Even though the strong ties of the Cuban family encourage young couples to live near their parents and to maintain intimate day-to-day relations, the establishment of an independent home continues to symbolize the beginning of married life. The extension of life expectancy, however, makes grandparents increasingly a part of family life. Some studies have shown that when two adult generations share a household traditional women's roles are reinforced; it may be that the grandmother's behavior contributes to the perpetuation of old patterns. When different generations live together, conflicts may arise, but at the same time grandparents' contributions in child care, shopping, and other chores may be significant. Much study remains to be done in this area.

In Cuba as in other Latin American countries, heads of families are predominantly male. Nevertheless, between 1970 and 1981 the percentage of male-headed households dropped from 57.2 to 50.0 percent while the percentage of female-headed households rose from 13.3 to 19.7 percent. This shift seems to be related to the increase in the divorce rate. The national demographic survey of 1979 showed that women represented 70.0 percent of divorced heads of households.

Marriage is the most prevalent form for establishment of a family, but consensual unions play an important role. Census data for 1953 and 1981 show little difference in the proportion of married (36.3 percent and 37.7 percent) and unmarried couples (19.1 percent and 20.4 percent). Studies have shown that consensual unions have become more important among the young (Catasús et al. 1987:57–58). The median age for first marriages or consensual unions declined between 1953 and 1970 but then remained steady through 1981. In 1953 the median age for men entering their first marriage or consensual union was 25.5 years, and in 1980–1981 it was 23.1 years; for women in 1953 the comparable age was 20.8, whereas in 1970 and 1981 it was 19.3, except in the rural areas, where it dropped to 18.7.

The increases in the divorce rate in the fifteen-to-twenty-four-year age-group and in the general prevalence of early marriages originating in the context of inadequate material conditions (economic dependency, lack of housing) and inadequate preparation for family life require further study to identify their causes and to develop policies to improve the quality of family life. The important role that the family plays in the formation of children's moral values and the need for this process to adjust to the progress of the revolutionary society in transition require that further analysis of these and related topics be included in future policy studies.

Notes

1. This analysis is part of the preliminary work for a major survey of the way of life of the Cuban family undertaken in the first half of 1989 by the Academy of Sciences of Cuba. The manuscript was completed in 1988.

2. Fertility is the number of children that a woman would have borne by the end of her fertile life under the assumption that the rates of fecundity by age of each cohort of women in a given year remain constant and mortality (of the women) does not intervene during the reproductive process.

3. The National Commission on Sexual Education and Family Life, adjunct to the Permanent Commission of the National Assembly on Childhood, Youth, and Equal Rights for Women, has been working in this direction since 1977 with some success; studies of adolescent sexual education are one result of this work.

4. In evaluating these data it is important to remember that the census of 1981 categorized as urban both communities with two thousand or more inhabitants and all inhabited areas with populations between five hundred and two thousand inhabitants that had public electricity and three or more of the following: sewers, paved streets, gutters, medical attention, and a school.

References

Álvarez, M., et al. 1987. *La madre soltera y la atención que recibe el hijo durante su primer año de vida.* Havana: Centro de Investigaciones Psicológicas y Sociológicas/Ministerio de Justicia.

Castro, Fidel. 1953. *La historia me absolverá.* Havana.

Catasús, S., et al. 1987. *La reproducción de la población y el desarrollo socioeconómico en Cuba.* Havana: Centro de Estudios Demográficos.

CEE (Comité Estatal de Estadísticas). 1981. *Censo de población y viviendas.* Vol. 16. Havana.

――――. 1986a. *Anuario Demográfico de Cuba.* Havana.

――――. 1986b. *Encuesta de presupuestos de tiempo.* Havana.

――――. n.d. *Encuesta demográfica nacional: Características de los núcleos y la familia.* Havana.

Código de familia. 1980. *Código de familia.* Havana: Orbe.

Colectivo de autores. 1987. *Sistematización y evaluación de la información disponible sobre la familia cubana.* Havana: Centro de Investigaciones Psicológicas y Sociológicas.

Domínguez, María Isabel. 1986. "La maternidad temprana en la Isla de Juventud. . . ." *Revista Santiago* 61 (March).

Espín, Vilma. 1986. "La batalla por el ejercicio pleno de la igualdad de la mujer: acción de comunistas." *Cuba Socialista* (20).

Farnós, A. 1979. "Características de la República de Cuba." *Revista Cubana de Administración de Salud* 6 (April-June).

_____. 1985. "La declinación de la fecundidad y sus perspectivas en el contexto de los procesos demográficos en Cuba." Thesis, Centro de Estudios Demográficos, Havana.

Fernández, L., et al. 1987. *El tiempo libre de la juventud en Cuba.* Havana: Abril.

González, F. 1986. *La participación de la mujer en la fuerza de trabajo y la fecundidad en Cuba.* Havana.

INSIE. 1979. *Encuesta de presupuestos de tiempo.* Havana.

PCC (Partido Comunista de Cuba). 1987. *Programa del Partido Comunista de Cuba.* Havana: Política.

13

Medical Applications of High Technology in Cuba

Manuel Limonta Vidal and Guillermo Padrón

Translated by Margaret Gilpin

January 1, 1959, marked the beginning of radical changes in the conception of the people's right to health. The new focus was the result of new social priorities that emphasized public health, its maintenance and preservation, the improvement of life expectancy, and a willingness to pursue these goals on an ongoing basis. Among the concrete objectives set forth were to broaden and improve the national health care system, focusing on prevention and health promotion, to ensure coverage of the entire population by a network of family doctors by the year 2000,[1] to continue to concentrate on maternal and child health and further reduce infant and maternal mortality, to continue to develop hygiene and epidemiology, to advance medical science and technology by incorporating the most modern preventive, diagnostic, and treatment methods, and to encourage research important for science and medical practice, particularly in tropical medicine, genetics, biotechnology, and prenatal diagnosis.

From the start, the revolutionary government began to develop broadly based programs of disease prevention. This required the training of large numbers of physicians and other health professionals to staff the many institutions providing health care services (Figure 13.1). This has resulted in 1 physician for every 302 inhabitants in a country with a population of 10.5 million. Medical facilities have gradually been constructed with the objective of providing service to all areas of the country. In December 1989 there were 263 hospitals, 11 research institutes, 420 polyclinics, 163 dental clinics, 239 medical posts, 3 spas, 148 maternity homes, and 23

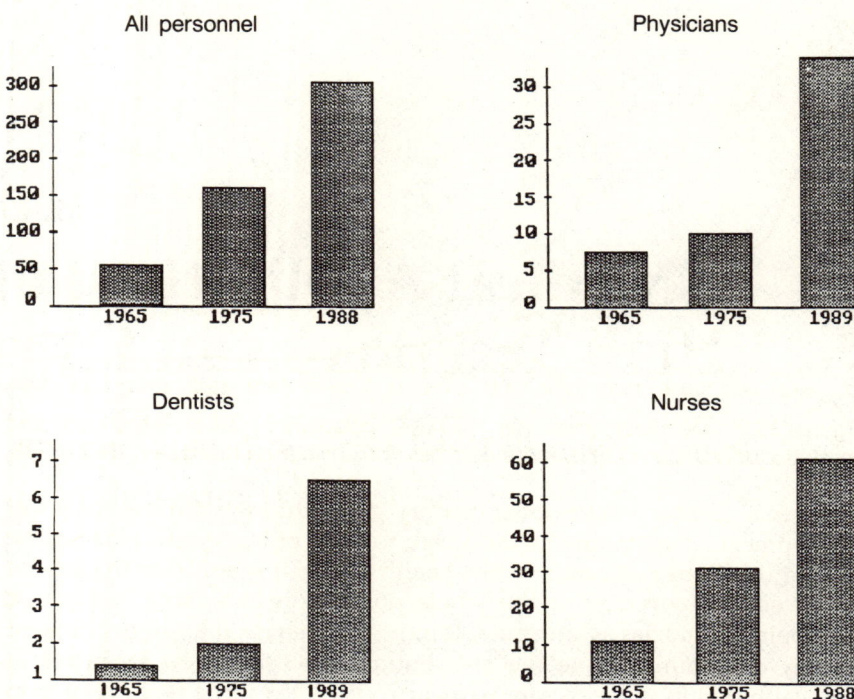

Figure 13.1   Health care personnel (thousands), 1965–1988.

blood banks. From 1959 to 1989 the number of hospital beds increased from 28,536 to 63,086 (MINSAP, 1990). Geographic regions were created to provide better preventive and treatment services and to strengthen institutional ties between different levels of the medical care system. These ties have allowed personnel in secondary and tertiary institutions to acquire intimate knowledge of the problems of primary care as part of a comprehensive development plan and a new work style resulting from an overall strategy for the country.

The priority given to health care has allowed Cuba to find ways to apply the major advances of modern science at different levels of medical care. Through optimal utilization of available resources and constant improvement in preventive medicine such as, for example, the attention given to pregnant women, the number of births in specialized institutions has progressively increased so that by 1989 99.8 percent of all births took place in hospitals. A 1972 article in the *New England Journal of Medicine*

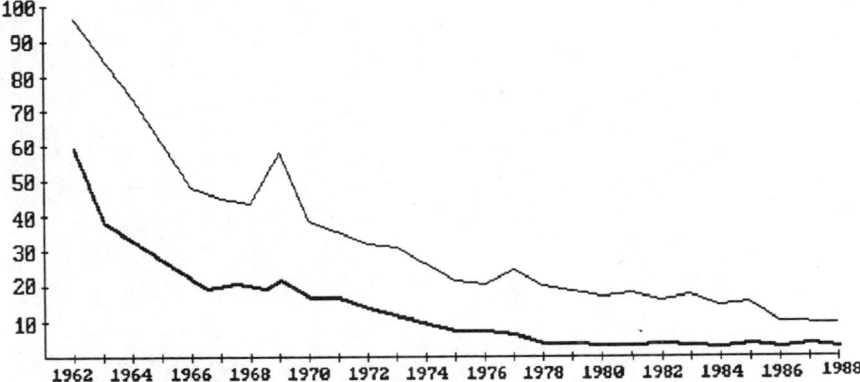

Figure 13.2 Mortality (rate per 100,000 population) from infectious and parasitic (upper curve) and acute diarrheal (lower curve) diseases, 1962–1988.

stated that "Cuba, a developing country going through difficult stages of development, is providing medical care to most of its people. And, in the light of the Cuban situation in the health sector, it seems that the lack of health service coverage of the whole population in a large number of developing countries is attributable not so much to the always present scarcity of resources as to the distribution of old and new resources in the health and in other sectors" (Navarro, 1972:959). The rapid reduction in mortality from infectious, parasitic, and acute diarrheas (Figure 13.2) and in perinatal mortality (Figure 13.3) achieved nationwide has resulted in illness and mortality rates typical of the developed world (Table 13.1). Life expectancy has also risen significantly, reaching 74.37 years in 1989. The superstructure and infrastructure that the revolution has built, together with sophisticated medical technology, have been the basis for this development.

Technological Development and Its Applications

From the first years of the postrevolutionary period, Cuba has emphasized and committed large quantities of resources to the application of high technology to the health problems of its population. In the process, it has created research institutes within and outside of the Ministry of Public Health that are charged with assimilating the latest advances of science and applying them free of charge to the entire population without distinction as to profession, race, creed, or class.

By the beginning of the 1960s Cuba was performing open-heart surgery, and between 1985 and 1989 there were 60 transplants, with 10 of the recipients surviving two years or more (MINSAP, 1990). By December

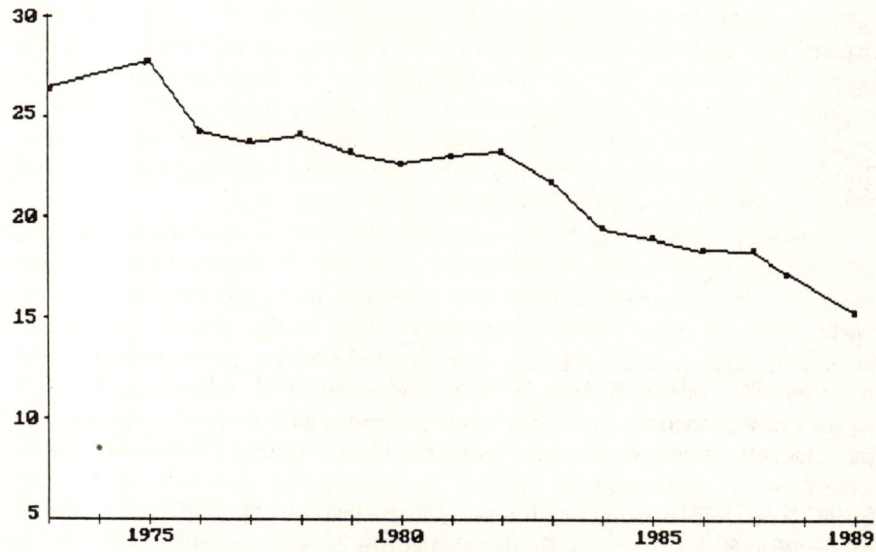

Figure 13.3   Perinatal mortality (deaths per 1,000 live births plus fetal deaths—1,000 g or more birthweight), 1975–1989.

TABLE 13.1   Main Causes of Death (per hundred thousand), All Ages, 1970–1988

Cause	1970	1980	1987	1988
Heart disease	148.6	166.7	185.5	191.8
Malignant neoplasm	98.9	106.6	119.7	124.7
Cerebrovascular disease	60.3	55.3	64.7	62.6
Accident	36.1	38.0	43.6	49.2
Influenza and pneumonia	42.1	38.6	39.3	31.4
Suicide and self-inflicted injury	11.8	21.4	22.4	21.3
Diabetes mellitus	9.9	11.1	17.0	20.8
Bronchitis, emphysema, and asthma	12.5	7.0	7.7	11.8
Certain perinatal conditions	41.7	13.2	10.8	9.4
Congenital anomalies	14.1	8.1	8.3	9.1

1989, Cuba had successfully transplanted 1,355 kidneys, 22 bone marrows, 10 livers, 3 pancreases, 19 pancreas-kidney combinations, 1 lung, 2 heart-lung combinations, and 789 corneas and had performed 80 neurotransplants (MINSAP, 1990). These figures are all the more impressive considering that they come from a small country whose access to scientific and technological information from the "most developed" country (the United States) has been blocked by the U.S. embargo. The blockade extends, incredibly, even to health and explicitly denies Cuban institutions access to developed technology.

One of the first achievements in the application of modern biotechnology in Cuba was the production and clinical use of interferon at the beginning of 1981. Part of the incentive for its development was the promise that it held as a treatment for cancer. At that time it was being produced in only eight or nine countries, all of them developed ones. Today Cuba continues to be the only Third World nation that produces forms of interferon consistently and in industrial form.

Interferon, obtained from white blood cells, was successfully introduced in June 1981 during an unrestrained epidemic of hemorrhagic dengue fever. Of the group of patients who received it, in contrast to controls, none died and none reached the critical stage of the illness (Limonta et al., 1983). This was the first study ever made of the use of interferon in the treatment of this illness. With its immediate and massive application to children in schools and other centers where children tend to congregate (and thereby create conditions favorable to contagion), Cuba was able to save the lives of dozens of children. Interferon has also been used with other viral and neoplastic illnesses, and despite the high price of the medication more than ten thousand people have been treated with it in Cuba, using different clinical protocols and always at no charge to the patient (Limonta, 1989).

Institutional Development

With the inauguration of the Centro Nacional de Investigaciones Científicas (National Center for Scientific Research, CNIC) in 1965, the basis was laid for accelerated scientific development and the introduction of the latest scientific and technological advances in the principal economic sectors of the country (sugar, cattle, mining, and food production), with preferential treatment being given to research related to human health. One of its functions was the organization and development of postgraduate training at the national level. The majority of Cuban scientists have been trained there, and many scientific institutes, such as the Centro Nacional de Salud Animal (National Center of Animal Health) and the Centro de Immunoensayo (Immunoassay Center, CIE), are outgrowths of CNIC.

Today CNIC's activities focus on the development of diagnostic techniques using advanced technology for the early detection of prevalent illnesses, the design and construction of high-technology medical equipment for automated diagnosis and procedures for its use, the introduction of in vitro cultivated human skin for the treatment of burn patients, the acquisition of active biological substances by extraction from natural sources and their biotransformation and chemical synthesis for use in medicines, the expansion of computer techniques to all spheres of scientific activity, and the modernization of electronic techniques and the development of families of equipment for use in research and health.

The center's results have permitted the establishment of a national program in clinical neurophysiology that uses high technology to explore nervous-system functions with a view to protecting at-risk groups in the population such as older people and high-risk newborns. To establish this program, a network is being created with no fewer than three laboratories in each of the fourteen provinces dedicated to neuropediatrics and adult neuropsychiatric diagnosis and to the identification and treatment of learning disorders. Fifteen of these laboratories are functioning in four provinces, and the rest should be completed by 1991. Their equipment was designed and constructed at CNIC, using technology and computers developed in Cuba because the blockade has made their acquisition in foreign markets impossible, and includes MEDICID-03M for electroencephalographs, NEURONICA-02 for measuring visual and audio perception and sleep waves, and NEUROCID-01 for electromyography. During the last four years of the development phase of this new technology, 97.3 percent of all newborns in Havana were screened for auditory defects (CNIC, 1989). This type of screening is only now beginning in a few of the developed countries of the world, and nowhere does it approach the coverage offered in Cuba.

Another important milestone was the inauguration in 1982 of the Centro de Investigaciones Biológicas (Center for Biological Research, CIB), a direct consequence of the achievements in the production and clinical use of interferon. When the necessity arose to find sources other than human blood for the production of interferon, genetic engineering became a goal for the center. By developing gene splicing, Cuba managed to substitute a highly efficient, low-cost, and easily available biotechnological process for a limited and generally costly natural source. With interferon as the model for experimentation, the technology was extended to other areas both within and outside the health field. Thus in 1985 CIB began to produce two new types of interferon that have given Cuba an arsenal of clinical treatments for a large number of viral and neoplastic illnesses (Limonta, 1986). Interferons obtained through genetic engineering had never before been produced by a Third World country.

Such meaningful results, achieved in such a short time, and the possibilities they presented were compelling reasons for constructing a center especially designed for genetic engineering and biotechnology. It was envisioned that this center would have the elements necessary to respond rapidly to the growing determination to explore all possibilities and to pursue the most advanced developments in world science. Embarking on such a project in 1984, at the height of the international economic crisis that was also affecting Cuba, was a step that required careful scientific evaluation and a good dose of courage and trust in the capacity of Cuban researchers.

On July 1, 1986, the Centro de Ingeniería Genética y Biotecnología (Center for Genetic Engineering and Biotechnology, CIGB) was opened in Havana. Constructed in two years on 15 hectares of land with buildings covering 70,000 square meters, the center comprised two principal buildings of eight stories each with laboratory and auxiliary installations, including high-security biological laboratories, refrigeration facilities, a four-hundred-seat auditorium for conferences and national and international scientific events, a production plant of 7,000 square meters, which is currently under expansion, animal stables (800 square meters), special housing for animals in controlled conditions, greenhouses for plant research, and a 112-room hotel for visiting scientists, postgraduate students, and other participants in scientific events.

Despite its brief existence, CIGB has already established a long tradition of sponsoring international workshops and conferences with broad foreign participation. This has allowed Cuba to contribute modestly to the world community. Notable among these events have been the first seminar on interferon, in which 700 delegates from 34 countries participated in 1983, the second seminar on interferon and the first on biotechnology, with the participation of 912 delegates from 44 countries in 1986, and the third seminar on interferon, the second on biotechnology, and the first Ibero-American congress on biotechnology in 1989, with the participation of 1,427 delegates from 51 countries.

If we analyze the results of the work of the collective at the CIGB (350 people) and the social benefits that have ensued, many of which relate directly to health, we see that the decision to make such a large investment was well worthwhile. CIGB has developed fifteen new substances, among them medicines, sophisticated diagnostic systems, and other substances for medical use. Obtained through genetic engineering, these substances have been employed in various national health-care programs. The efforts of the center have led to the production not only of recombinant Alpha and Gamma interferons but of three proteins of the AIDS virus capable of being used to diagnose carriers of the disease. Cuba has screened a greater percentage of its population for AIDS than any country in the hemisphere except the United States, Canada, and Mexico (OPS, 1989a). As of November 1989, 5,495,247 tests had been carried out, resulting in the detection of 333 HIV seropositives (carriers) and 80 active cases, of which 17 have ended in death. The availability of a third-generation diagnostic system, combined with other programmatic factors, enabled Cuba in 1989 to have the lowest rate of infection in the Americas (0.004 percent of the tested population). This modern diagnostic method has been achieved in only six other countries, all in the developed world.

Recombinant epidermal growth factor is another medicine obtained through genetic engineering and now produced industrially at CIGB. Discovered only a few years ago, it is capable of considerably accelerating the regeneration of human skin. A wide variety of applications for its use have already been discovered, ranging from the treatment of vascular ulcers to that of diabetes and leprosy. In the treatment of burn victims functional skin recovery has been achieved in less than half the conventional time. Only four other countries (all developed) have produced this medicine, and Cuba was the first to register it for medicinal uses.

Currently CIGB is producing a total of 136 different products, among which are 15 new proteins and 40 types of monoclonal antibodies (representing the most advanced generation of immunological applications to different problems in diagnosis and treatment). Together, all the other countries of Latin America only produce 40 monoclonal antibodies. Cuba has also produced a series of substances necessary for specialized laboratory work such as enzyme restriction and the modification of nucleic acids, the reagents employed for work in genetic engineering. CIGB produces 40 different enzymes, about double that produced in all the other countries of Latin America, in addition to other types of medicine, biological reagents, and diagnostics.

The Centro de Immunoensayo, opened in September 1987, is responsible for developing diagnostic techniques based on immunochemical methodology, using an ultramicroanalytic system called the Sistema Ultra Microanalítico (SUMA) that employs a much smaller quantity of reagents than other systems and is therefore much less costly. Relying upon Cuban equipment and reagents has been the only economical way to carry out the SUMA-based diagnostic programs on the scale at which they have been implemented. The installation of SUMA in all Cuban blood banks has permitted individual AIDS and hepatitis B screening and, among others, eleven additional tests. Because of its success, the SUMA group now has its own center.

The CIE has made a considerable contribution to improving the health of the Cuban people. In 1988, 91.1 percent of all pregnant women were tested prenatally for the most important congenital anomalies, such as neural tube defects (CIE, 1989). From 1982 to 1989 a total of 4,258 positives were diagnosed, allowing each couple the right to interrupt the pregnancy if it so desired and thus reducing maternal risk and the resultant high social costs. Similar programs have been established in Sweden and the United States, but they cover only part of the at-risk population and only privately. In England a program of this type was initiated but eventually discontinued.

SUMA is also used to screen for congenital hypothyroidism. Thanks to screening of newborns, a total of 74 cases have been detected and treated, thereby avoiding the development of the illness and the severe psychomotor retardation that accompanies it. A total of 141,922 newborns were tested, establishing the incidence at 1 per 2,500 live births (CIE, 1989). A similar program has been initiated in Japan but on a much smaller scale. These successes permit the targeting of new and more ambitious goals, such as the use of SUMA to evaluate allergy sensitivity in newborns (until now the only program of its kind in the world) and to screen for leprosy, viral respiratory diseases, and parasitic and infectious diseases with a view to their eradication.

The Centro de Neurotransplante y Regeneración del Sistema Nervioso (Center for Neurotransplants and Regeneration of the Nervous System), opened at the beginning of 1989, has a multidisciplinary staff of neurosurgeons, biochemists, immunologists, pathologists, biologists, and related specialists who do research on nervous-system disorders such as Parkinson's disease and on spinal cord lesions. They have performed 100 operations, including 27 epiploon transpositions to correct sequelae of stroke, 17 for spinal cord injuries, and 2 for craniofacial trauma. In addition, they have done 29 transplants of fetal substantia nigra to treat the symptoms of Parkinson's syndrome, with patients experiencing 100 percent recovery. The Parkinson's surgery has been done in Mexico and Sweden and twice in the United States.

The Centro Nacional de Biopreparados (National Center for Biopreparations, CNB) and the Centro de Vacunas (Vaccine Center) have managed, despite their different foci, to use molecular biology to benefit public health. Working with CIGB, they have developed the world's first vaccine against meningococcal meningitis, with highly satisfactory results, as well as various diagnostic kits.

In addition to these institutions that directly support the application of high technology to health problems in Cuba, others play an important role and deserve to be mentioned: The Cardiocentral Infantil (Pediatric Cardiocenter) is part of a national network of six cardiocenters. Opened in 1986, it is the only institution of its kind providing high-level medical care to children. As of September 30, 1989, it had performed 1,339 complex and specialized cardiac operations, of which 712 were open-heart, with a survival rate of 86.16 percent. The center, using high technology, offers diagnostic services for cardiac congenital malformations, both pre- and postnatally, and has performed 17,743 tests, 1,700 of them prenatally. It has a thirty-bed postoperative and rehabilitation facility. The Instituto Nacional de Oncología y Radiobiología (National Institute of Oncology and Radiobiology) has done important work in the diagnosis and treatment of cancers and produces various types of monoclonal antibodies. The Instituto de Medicina Tropical "Pedro Kouri" (Pedro Kouri Institute of Tropical Medicine) provides clinical service, teaching, and research in the field of tropical diseases, using epidemiology and biotechnology. A new complex to house the institute is under construction. The Centro Nacional para la Producción de Animales de Laboratorio (National Center for the Production of Laboratory Animals) is dedicated to providing animals for scientific research. Here, too, a new center is under construction.

Other institutions that participate in these important activities include the general medical and surgical hospital Hermanos Almeijeras, where the sixty heart transplants mentioned earlier were performed, the national institutes of hematology and immunology, gastroenterology, cardiology and cardiovascular surgery, and angiology, the Calixto García hospital, and the Centro de Investigaciones Médico-quirúrgicas (Center for Medical and Surgical Research). These institutions are closely tied to each other and to various preventive and treatment programs coordinated by the Ministry of Public Health. They also participate in groups such as the Frente Biológica (Biological Front), an organization created in 1981 by Fidel Castro with the goal of defining work priorities for research, laboratories, and production in biology and reconciling national needs with the country's capacity to respond to them.

In this necessarily brief summary of the results achieved and the institutions directly involved in procuring higher health levels and improving the quality of life, some things of importance may have been omitted.

Conclusion

A country's possibilities for developing science and biotechnology depend on its level of development and its political will and economic organization. Since biotechnology in the developed world is essentially based on private investment motivated by profit, the Third World is in a disadvantageous and dependent situation. Cuba is an exception; because its growth and problem solving are based on scientific concepts, it has achieved a higher level of scientific and biotechnological development than any other Third World country. The Pan American Health Organization notes that this has occurred precisely during a period of economic crisis in which "the available resources for the public health sector have diminished in the same proportion as total public expenditures" (OPS, 1989b). Almost all of these important scientific achievements have served other peoples of the world, and more than twenty countries have directly benefited from the products, equipment, and techniques developed in Cuba from the so-called high technologies. Cubans view these achievements as the result of a revolution in education, technology, and society combined with the political will to ensure that the utmost attention is given to the welfare of the people.

Notes

1. This is the national program of primary care that guarantees a doctor for every 120 families. Family physicians live and work in the communities they serve.

References

CIE (Centro de Immunoensayo). 1989. *Sistema ultramicroanalítico: resultados de los principales programas de aplicación, resumen, diciembre, 1989.* Havana.

CNIC (Centro Nacional de Investigaciones Científicas). 1989. *"Neurosciences '80": International Conference on Advanced Methods in Neurosciences, February 1989.* Havana.

Limonta, Manuel. 1986. "Revisión de los ensayos clínicos con interferón en Cuba." Report on the Second Cuban Seminar on Interferon and the First Cuban Seminar on Biotechnology, Havana, April.

———. 1989. "Revisión de los ensayos clínicos con interferón en Cuba." Speech given at the Third Cuban and International Seminar on Interferon, the Second Cuban and International Seminar on Biotechnology, and the First Ibero-American Congress on Biotechnology, Havana, April.

Limonta, Manuel, et al. 1983. "Uso del interferón leucocitario durante una epidemia de dengue hemorrágico (virus tipo II) en Cuba." *Interferón y Biotechnología* 1 (3):15–22.

MINSAP (Ministerio de Salud Pública). 1990. *Informe anual de 1989.* Havana.

Navarro, V. 1972. "Health services in Cuba: An initial appraisal." *New England Journal of Medicine* 287:959.

OPS (Organización Panamericana de Salud). 1989a. *Síndrome de inmunodeficiencia adquirida en las Américas.* Document No. CD34/13:25. Washington, D.C.

———. 1989b. *Salud y desarrollo: repercuciones de la crisis económica.* Document No. CE103/7:8. Washington, D.C.

14

Thirty Years of Cuban Revolutionary Penal Law

Raúl Gómez Treto

Law is not simply the contents of a code or official gazette; it is or should be the most important ethical and political instrument for the preservation of social peace and the promotion of a new social order. It is, furthermore, not merely the formal implementation of the will of the dominant class, for if it is to remain effective it must correspond to the social and material conditions of life. The law reflects the social behavior accepted and engaged in by the majority of the population of a society, and at the same time it delineates the boundary between good and bad for the peaceful development of that society.

In a democratic society, the law governs the behavior of every citizen, the ruler as well as the ruled. Although the issue is disputed abroad, at home the majority of the Cuban people have opted for socialism—in spite of all its shortcomings and risks—as the only route to a truly democratic society. The law publicly sets forth the acceptable standard of behavior so that everyone can be aware of and conform to it; at the same time, it warns that behavior in violation of that standard will be counteracted if possible and any damage from it mandatorily compensated. There are, however, certain acts that, independent of any direct damage they may cause, in themselves create a form of social disorder that requires additional punishment to prevent its repetition.

Historically, legal punishment has ranged from pure and brutal revenge to some variant of reeducation. In extreme cases, however, social reeducation (general prevention) requires such severe personal punishment as the death penalty or life imprisonment—measures intended to discourage others from committing the crime rather than reeducating the violator. The legal system that deals with these acts is penal law; complementary to this are what is called penitentiary law and a number of other legal subsystems (civil, labor, economic, administrative, and so on). This chapter examines how the penal law of the Cuban Revolution has changed over time.

The Spanish penal code had been the basis for the rule of law in Cuba since 1879, long before the country became a republic (Código penal, 1922). It was a classic continental code that included the death penalty and life imprisonment for several crimes. Although manipulated in various ways (even in Europe, in the direction of fascism), it was apparently progressive and served as the inspiration for the social defense code. Adopted in 1936, this code not only included the death penalty and up to thirty years (instead of life) imprisonment but introduced pre- and postoffense detention. Only in 1940, when many Cubans anticipated a long period of democracy and peace, was a constitution adopted that limited the use of the death penalty (Constitución, 1940).[1] It should be noted, however, that during the short period in which the death penalty was limited, the most scandalous crimes, including brutal assassinations and terrorism, were committed by the Batista dictatorship. This and other problems were confronted in the new penal code under the revolution.

Revolutionary Penal Law: Severity and Effectiveness

A revolution is an acceleration of the historical rhythm of a society. The law, as a political and ethical instrument, very clearly reflects the society's development and transformation. Penal law, as an exceptional political instrument for the control of social behavior, is at the same time a barometer of social change. This is especially true in a revolutionary period. Cuban revolutionary penal law, along with other instruments, has been used in various ways to help build a socialist system of social relations.

During the rebellion against Fulgencio Batista's dictatorship, the general command of the rebel army, led by Fidel Castro, introduced into the liberated territories the nineteenth-century penal law commonly known as the Ley de la Sierra.[2] This law included the death penalty for extremely serious crimes, whether perpetrated by the dictatorship or by supporters of the revolution. In 1959 the revolutionary government extended its application to the whole of the republic and to war criminals captured and tried after the war of liberation. This latter extension, supported by the majority of the population, followed the same procedure as that seen in the trials held by the Allies in Nuremberg after World War II.

Fulfilling one of Fidel Castro's promises to the people in his revolutionary program (Castro, 1973:63), a Fundamental Law was enacted to restore as much as possible the Constitution of 1940 (Ley fundamental, 1959). One change, however, was the cancellation of the limitation on the death penalty. Those who were in Cuba at the time are well aware that if the revolutionary government had not applied severe legislation against the few hundred torturers, bombers, and other brutal criminals long employed by the Batista regime, the people themselves would have taken justice into their own hands—as happened during the anti-Machado rebellion—and thrown the society into chaos. It was only the population's confidence in the government's effective—and cautiously selective—administration of "revolutionary justice" that kept the society in order. Even many who, for various reasons, do not consider the death penalty an effective remedy for criminality have acknowledged that in such an extraordinary situation the severity of the penal law was justified or, at least, forgivable.[3] The death penalty was imposed on enemies of the people, those who had killed, tortured, assassinated, and committed genocide during the war and continued to conspire against the revolution—who had supported and participated in the Batista dictatorship and feared fulfillment of the revolutionary promise of an end to class privilege, exploitation, and the abuses of so-called republican democracy maintained by the former Cuban bourgeoisie, American corporations, and the U.S. government.

Just when one would have thought that punitive justice had been sufficient to discourage any further brutality in Cuban history, Cuban territory was invaded in 1961 by an army financed, trained, and supported by a foreign state. Defeated in less than seventy-two hours by the joint forces of the rebel army, the revolutionary police, and the people's voluntary national militia, the war prisoners, almost all of them being Cuban citizens perpetrating military aggression against their own country under foreign patronage, were tried. Although they could have been condemned to death, all except certain former war criminals who had earlier escaped revolutionary justice under the same foreign patronage were merely sentenced to imprisonment. Revolutionary penal law was very severe, but its application was extremely selective.

The immediate reaction of the revolution's enemies was to initiate a long period of minor military infiltration, creating and developing guerrilla bands in various mountainous parts of the country parallel to the terrorists and saboteurs in the cities. Military action was required to put an end to this new kind of aggression, seen in continual crimes against peasants, rural teachers, ordinary workers and citizens, government officials, and revolutionary leaders, including (as was later acknowledged by the U.S. government) assassination attempts against Castro himself. The penal law had to be employed with the utmost severity (including the application of the death penalty in several cases) against the enemy agents captured. It must be noted that in spite of the seriousness of the crimes, the death penalty was generally imposed only in the most extreme cases rather than in all the cases that technically called for it.

During these years, political attacks frequently occurred under the cover of ordinary crimes. This forced the government to develop very detailed and complicated penal laws, with amendments to cover all kinds of acts against life, health, ecology, property, and so on, and eventually to collect and systematize these in a new penal code.

In spite of Cuban socialism's emphasis on the educational function of punishment, the extent of criminality during the period just described had led Cuban specialists and politicians to conclude that some severity was required.[4] Therefore, the penal code adopted by the National Assembly in 1979, although affirming the educational function of punishment as its theoretical foundation (Código penal, 1979), defined many punishable acts and established higher levels of punishment than the 1936 code and its complementary laws. In a way it summed up the measures employed in the preceding years against the continual assaults suffered by the revolutionary people. The publication of the code was taken by the enemies of the people as an opportunity to brand the revolution as excessively repressive and cruel. As I have pointed out elsewhere, the counterrevolution was right in criticizing the penal law of those years: It was so efficient that it stopped almost all direct counterrevolutionary actions.

Depenalization

By 1979, in the light of trends in the penal sciences in important parts of the world, it was recognized that instead of stopping or reducing criminality we were "producing" criminals in Cuba.[5] This contradictory effect of our penal law was in part the result of the fact that it had until then been used to punish counterrevolutionary actions consciously or unconsciously concealed behind what appeared to be ordinary crimes. In the new situation, instead of punishing counterrevolutionary agents we found that we were punishing ordinary workers and citizens, some of them from the best revolutionary backgrounds, who had engaged in various forms of antisocial behavior for reasons far from any counterrevolutionary intention. Most of the time the antisocial actions then considered crimes resulted from a lack of civic or political education and from the scarcity of consumer goods due to the economic embargo and blockade imposed on our country by powerful foreign enemies of the revolution. By punishing ordinary Cuban workers as if they were enemies, we were failing to help reeducate them. Analysis of this contradictory situation led to a reconsideration of the whole state response to criminality. Out of this came the conclusion that instead of harsh punishment what was needed were legal mechanisms to preserve social order by effectively reeducating those who had engaged in serious antisocial behavior.

Misdemeanors, which had been considered minor crimes under the penal laws of 1870 and 1936, were excluded from the penal code of 1979 and covered by special legislation of an administrative nature. Under this legislation the most serious offenses received the highest fine, 50 pesos, and most fines were less than 20 pesos (Decreto-ley, 1979, 1984, 1987). The philosophy was not to punish severely but to persuade people "not to do it again" until it was possible to teach them "not to do it any more." The procedure whereby these fines were imposed included an appeal process. This system was intended to cover minor offenses in every field of social life (ecology, health, economy, education, public order, and so on), but it must be said that it has not yet been completed. The difficulty of avoiding punishing an act more than once has delayed the enforcement of the complementary decrees that would cover every area of social and economic activity. It has, however, been implemented in some areas with good results and has been improved through successive amendments. Many kinds of antisocial acts once considered minor criminal offenses have become misdemeanors in this process of depenalization.

Many breaches of social and economic discipline that during the "hard years" were included in the penal law have been transferred to the first labor code (Código de trabajo, 1985) through various measures designed to induce workers to maintain social, labor, and economic order. Considering that the new Cuban society is fundamentally composed of rural and urban workers whose good or bad behavior is reflected not only on the job but also in their families, homes, and neighborhoods, correcting any deviation helps to spread this educational influence without having to appeal to more severe forms of punishment. Labor-discipline measures range from a simple private or public admonition through demotion to dismissal. Care is taken to guarantee that a worker required to pay a fine because of a misdemeanor at work does not automatically suffer a labor-discipline measure for the first offense. One who has been corrected by a labor-discipline measure will not be fined as long as he or she does not repeat the infraction.

It is a universal rule that anyone who causes economic damage to another through criminal behavior, failure to fulfill a contract, or simple negligence must render compensation for it. A new civil code (Código civil, 1987) includes some important differences in this respect in that it reflects new social conditions. Given that Cuban society is composed of people who depend on salaries, wages, social security or assistance, and savings, it is clear that they cannot pay compensation for damage (e.g., to a ship, a plane, a factory, and so on) that would amount to millions of pesos. Moreover, it is recognized that the society and the state are partly responsible for the offender's irresponsibility, and therefore the new civil code contains limitations on personal liability. Instead of the whole amount of the damage, offenders must pay only a proportion of their income over a number of years, the remainder of the debt to be absorbed by the national, local, or enterprise budget. In addition, offenders' superiors must render labor, administrative, or even civil account for employing irresponsible workers by compensating the budget. While this may be considered a fairer way of handling liability, this new code includes the new concept of "objective responsibility"—the idea that indemnity for any damage must be paid to the extent possible in accordance with the above-mentioned proportions and limits. Experience has demonstrated that many antisocial actions can be discouraged in this simple way.

Review of closed penal judicial cases now allows the reopening of any case to determine whether there were mistakes, excessive severity, or other grounds for alteration of the sentence in favor of the convicted individual. As is usual in socialist societies, which have no such institution as amnesty, this process substitutes for pardon. Within a few years of this decree, almost half of the prison population had been released either entirely or on parole, which reflects both the formal severity of the old law in contrast to the new more humane one and the change in the definition of criminality.[6]

The penal code of 1971 was revised in 1987 to incorporate the depenalization just described. In summary, the new code (Código penal, 1987) redefines certain behaviors as misdemeanors or simply violations of labor discipline, eliminates the death penalty as a possible punishment for certain crimes (while retaining it for a limited number of others), reduces some of the maximum or minimum limits of possible imprisonment, eliminates the possibility of punishing with fines instead of imprisonment in several cases, eliminates the possibility of punishing with imprisonment and fines in others, reduces the level of fines in many others, and—what is very interesting—gives the courts the freedom to punish with new alternatives to imprisonment. A few new crimes are defined, however, particularly acts by government officials, and the limits of possible prison sentences and fines are increased in a few instances. In addition, a military penal law (Ley de los delitos militares, 1979)—more severe, of course, than that applied to civilians—regulates offenses perpetrated by members of the armed forces or the Ministry of the Interior.

In addition to the penal code, the penitentiary system was recognized as presenting opportunities for reeducation. The prisons inherited by the Cuban Revolution were very old—most of them old Spanish fortresses—

and inadequate. During the first revolutionary years there were other priorities (e.g., schools, universities, hospitals, factories, roads, and dams), including military construction in response to the attacks and threats of enemies of the revolution. After twenty to twenty-five years of developing that infrastructure, a new kind of prison was needed and began to be built.[7] At the same time, improvements were made in the training of guards and advisory and auxiliary personnel. All these developments were aimed at completing the work of reeducation of convicts as an essential goal of a socialist society in which, for moral and humanitarian but also economic and practical reasons, delinquents and antisocial minorities are to be helped to become productive workers.

Finally, since delinquency is a social ill, it must be not only cured but also prevented. In 1986, Comisiones de Prevención y Atención Social (Commissions for Social Attention and Prevention) were organized at the national, provincial, municipal, and even town and village levels (Decreto-ley, 1986). Composed of teachers, professors, lawyers, and other professionals who can contribute to delinquency prevention among our children and youngsters, these commissions attempt not only to compensate for a lack of ordinary care among youth but also to assist families, groups, and individuals (e.g., released convicts, the mentally retarded, the ill, and the handicapped). They have the official collaboration of state institutions and the voluntary cooperation of all mass organizations. Their methods of operation are not judiciary; they seek out conflict situations and pursue the best practical solutions for them, and only when mediation fails will a case be taken to the state administrative or judicial authorities.

Evaluation

The above account demonstrates, first, that during the initial period the penal instrument, though exceptional, was frequently and severely used to channel the people's fury against war criminals and to combat attempts to destabilize the revolutionary order under the cover of ordinary crimes. This severity proved sufficient to reduce—if not completely eliminate—the increasing criminality of those years. Most of that criminality was either a remnant of class society, which cultivated illiteracy, discrimination, poverty, and violence, or a counterrevolutionary effort to create obstacles to the country's peaceful and progressive development.

Obviously, it cannot be said that at the height of the antisocial violence and counterviolence provoked by the defenders of the old social system justice was done in every case. The later punishment of police, government officials, judges, military personnel, and others is evidence of the recognition by the state, the government, and the various political authorities of their excesses, in keeping with the patriotic tradition exhibited since the nineteenth-century wars of independence. The punitive approach of the revolutionary government in that period was a defensive reaction to the criminal initiatives of the defeated exploiters of our people. Once counterrevolutionary criminal violence had diminished and the government had discovered that a high level of punishment was not only unnecessary but damaging to the social order and the people's interest, a process of depenalization was initiated.

Whereas punishment was in some cases excessive, especially considering the lack of prevention, the undeveloped penitentiary system of reeducation and so on, depenalization also has its critics; some Cubans consider it the cause of the recent upsurge of criminality. After the most recent criminal scandals (the Ochoa and Abrantes trials) there were calls for repenalization of acts whose previous penalization had been reduced. Something must and will be done about this but not emotionally or demagogically.

Cuba needs and appreciates international solidarity, but it has received it only from some countries and parts of the world while suffering the lack of it and every kind of aggression from others. Despite being small, poor, exploited, and constantly under attack, it has survived and improved its social standing in the past thirty years through socialism and the constant rectification of errors. In the light of this, penalization and depenalization in its legal system can be expected to depend more on the treatment received from outside than on the Cuban people's wishes. As I have said elsewhere,

> Weapons should not exist, but the existence of enemies of justice and peace requires the regrettable effort of building them. They should not be used except to neutralize the unjust acts of those enemies when this cannot be done by other means. Weapons can be eliminated when the reduction of hostility allows it, but they cannot be destroyed while the enemy exists and continues to act. Meanwhile, penal law is a legal weapon of exceptional efficiency in the defense of social justice and peace. (Gómez Treto, 1985:149)

Notes

1. Its Article 25 specified that the death penalty would not be imposed except for military offenses by members of the armed forces and treason or espionage in time of war against a foreign nation.

2. The penal law of the War of Independence (July 28, 1896) was reinforced by Rule 1 of the penal regulations of the rebel army, approved in the Sierra Maestra February 21, 1958, and published in the army's official bulletin (Ley penal de Cuba en armas, 1959).

3. From 1959 to 1987 237 death sentences were handed down, mostly during the first years of the revolution, and all but 21 were carried out. No woman has

ever been executed. Since the single execution for a crime against state security in 1984 there have been no executions of this kind; their number had been six in 1980, three in 1981, one in 1982, and two in 1983. There were seven executions for ordinary offenses in 1984, one in 1985, none in 1986, and three in 1987. In 1986–1987, eleven convicts awaiting the death penalty were pardoned (cf. Amnesty International, 1989).

4. Different doctrinal positions have been taken in Cuba and in other socialist countries (for reviews, see Quiros Pires, 1986; Cejas Sánchez, 1986; Barrios Veguez, 1986; Mendoza Díaz, 1989). Most socialist specialists favor the doctrine of "dangerousness," but some prefer the doctrine of social "harmfulness" or "noxiousness" (cf. Kuznetzova, 1984).

5. In presenting the draft of the new penal code to the 3rd Session (December 1987) of the National Assembly the minister of the interior said, "It is indisputable that there were mistakes in the conception of our present penal code (1979) and in the number of offenses that were included. . . . The most dangerous offenses still perpetrated in Cuba today are against property, especially robbery by force and robbery with violence or intimidation. . . . Offenses against the (social) economy and against life and personal integrity constitute a minor proportion. . . . Minor offenses such as theft have registered some increase in recent years." He offered the following figures for the period 1980–1986: Of 1,500,000 cases, only 10.2 percent were serious offenses; 51.7 percent were thefts, traffic violations, and assaults. Of the 266,000 thefts, 90 percent were of less than $100. Of the 227,000 traffic violations, 92.5 percent involved driving without a license or driving having consumed alcohol (but not drunk; no injuries or damages). Of the 200,000 assaults, 95 percent were the result of simple quarrels with no further consequences.

6. Unofficial statistics indicate a recidivism rate of only 4 percent after two years and 6 percent after four.

7. Contrary to some reports, the building of new and better prisons began in the 1970s for humanitarian, social, moral, and internal political reasons rather than to prepare for the visits of foreigners and international commissions in the 1980s (cf. Amnesty International, 1988).

References

Amnesty International. 1988. "Cuba: Recent developments affecting the situation of political prisoners and the use of the death penalty." *AI Index* (September).

———. 1989. "Cuando es el estado el que mata . . . ," in *Los derechos humanos frente a la pena de muerte*. Madrid.

Barrios Veguez, Raúl. 1986. "Algunas consideraciones sobre la peligrosidad social." *Revista Cubana de Derecho* (27):51–58.

Castro, Fidel. 1973. *La historia me absolverá*. Havana: Ciencias Sociales Instituto Cubano del Libro.

Cejas Sánchez, Antonio. 1986. "Algunas consideraciones sobre la peligrosidad social." *Revista Cubana de Derecho* (27):43–50.

184   *Raúl Gómez Treto*

Código civil. 1987. No. 59 (July 16). *Gaceta Oficial Extraordinaria* No. 9 (October 15).

Código de defensa social. 1936. No. 802 (April 4). *Gaceta Oficial Ordinaria* No. 108 (April 11).

Código de trabajo. 1985. No. 49 (December 28, 1984). *Gaceta Oficial Ordinaria* No. 2 (February 23).

Código penal. 1922. Edited by Angel C. Betancourt. Havana.

––––––. 1979. No. 21 (February 15). *Gaceta Oficial Ordinaria* No. 3 (March 1).

––––––. 1987. No. 62 (December 29). *Gaceta Oficial Especial* No. 3 (December 30).

Constitución de la República de Cuba. 1940. *Gaceta Oficial Ordinaria* No. 646 (July 8).

Decreto-ley. 1979. No. 27 (October 27). *Gaceta Oficial Extraordinaria* (No. 12 (October 29).

––––––. 1984. No. 80 (March 28). *Gaceta Oficial Extraordinaria* No. 6 (March 29).

––––––. 1985. No. 87 (July 22). *Gaceta Oficial Extraordinaria*.

––––––. 1986. No. 95 (August 29). *Gaceta Oficial Especial* No. 7 (September 1).

––––––. 1987. No. 99 (December 25). *Gaceta Oficial Extraordinaria* No. 12 (December 25).

Gómez Treto, Raúl. 1985. "La nueva legislación cubana de infracciones administrativas." *Revista Jurídica* (9):7–162.

Kuznetzova, Nadezhna F. 1984. *El perfeccionamiento de las normas jurídicas sobre los delitos.* Moscow: Nauka.

Ley de los delitos militares. 1979. No. 22 (February 15). *Gaceta Oficial Ordinaria* (March 5).

Ley fundamental de la República. 1959. *Gaceta Oficial Extraordinaria* No. 13 (February 7).

Ley penal de Cuba en armas. 1959. *Leyes penales de la Revolución,* vol. 4, *Cuaderno extraordinario* (March):11–40, 41–79. Havana: Lex.

Mendoza Díaz, Juan R. 1989. "Estado peligroso: Breve análisis," in *Enfoques jurídicos de abogados cubanos.* Havana.

Quiros Pires, Renén. 1986. "Despenalización." *Revista Jurídica* (10):125–153.

About the Book

Since the rectification period of 1985–1986, Cuban scholars have been engaged in ongoing analysis of the political and social agendas of contemporary Cuba. In this volume, leading Cuban scholars explore several controversial themes, including the relation between democracy and socialism, strategies for economic development, and patterns of social change.

Taking into account the difficulties Cuba faces as it confronts changing international trade relations and diminishing aid following the breakup of the Soviet Union, contributors examine specific economic problems, such as the large external debt and shortages of material goods. They also address various aspects of domestic life in Cuba, including the youth movement and gender roles. Finally, they offer retrospective views of the Cuban Revolution—its origins; its accomplishments in the areas of health care, education, and social services; and obstacles to the realization of its ideological objectives.

About the Contributors
and Translators

Contributors

Juan Antonio Blanco specializes in the history of international relations and is a collaborator of the Centro de Estudios sobre América in Havana.

Julio Carranza Valdés is subdirector of the Centro de Estudios sobre América in Havana. His paper was originally presented at a discussion sponsored by the Instituto Nicaragüense de Investigación y Estudios Sociales (INIES) and appeared in *Boletín Socioeconómico* 16 (January-March 1990) in Managua.

Haroldo Dilla is a researcher in the Department of Caribbean Studies at the Centro de Estudios sobre América in Havana and the author of numerous articles on Cuban affairs.

Miguel Alejandro Figueras is advisor to the Comité Estatal de Colaboración Económica and adjunct titular professor at the University of Havana. He has been director of planning in the Ministry of Industry, vice-minister of the Sugar Industry, and first vice-president of the Central Office of Planning. He has published a book and more than twenty articles on various economic themes.

Raúl Gómez Treto received his doctor of law degree from the University of Havana in 1954 and is a senior legal advisor to the Cuban Ministry of Justice. He is also president of the Cuban Society of Civil and Family Law.

Armando Hart Dávalos is the Cuban Minister of Culture and author of numerous books and articles on Cuban affairs.

Rafael Hernández is chair of the Department of North American Studies at the Centro de Estudios sobre América in Havana. In 1989 he was a visiting scholar at the Center for International Affairs at Harvard University. He has published numerous articles about U.S.-Cuban relations and coauthored, with Jorge Domínguez, *U.S.–Cuban Relations in the Nineties* (Boulder: Westview, 1989).

Manuel Limonta Vidal is general director of the Centro de Ingeniería y Biotecnología in Havana.

Juan Luis Martín in a researcher with the Academy of Sciences in Havana.

Fernando Martínez Heredia is chair of the Department of Regional Studies at the Centro de Estudios sobre América in Havana. He is the author of numerous books and articles on Cuban affairs.

Guillermo Padrón is an engineer-researcher at the Centro de Ingeniería Genética y Biotecnología in Havana.

Inés Cristina Reca is affiliated with the Centro de Investigaciones Psicológicas y Sociológicas of the Cuban Academy of Sciences.

José Luis Rodríguez García is assistant director of the Centro de Investigaciones de la Economía Mundial in Havana and specializes in the economy of socialist countries. His most recent work is *La estrategia de desarrollo económico de la revolutión cubana* (Havana: Ciencias Sociales, 1990).

Georgina Suárez Hernández teaches philosophy at the Escuela Superior del Partido Comunista de Cuba "Nico López" and is a member of its scientific council. Her area of research is the internal politics of the Cuban Revolution.

Carlos Tablada is an economist who has worked in the management of Cuban state enterprises. His book *Che Guevara and Politics in the Transition to Socialism* (1989) was awarded the Ernesto Che Guevara special prize in the 1987 Casa de las Américas literary competition.

Translators

Diana Alarcón is a doctoral candidate in political economy and international development in the Department of Economics at the University of California, Riverside.

Michael Baumann is associated with Pathfinder Press, New York.

James Bloyd is a public health worker for the County of Los Angeles.

Jean Díaz is a graduate student in the Department of Political Science at the University of California, Riverside.

Jennifer Dugan Abbassi is a coordinating editor of *Latin American Perspectives* and a doctoral candidate in the Department of Political Science at the University of California, Riverside.

Margaret Gilpin is a specialist on family health care and has published articles on Cuba's health system. She resides in Cuba and is affiliated with the Albert Einstein College of Medicine in the Bronx, New York.

Terry McKinley is a doctoral candidate in political economy and international development in the Department of Economics of the University of California, Riverside.

Philip R. Martínez is a graduate student in the Department of Economics at the University of California, Riverside.

Janell Pierce recently graduated from the University of California, Riverside, with a B.A. in Latin American Studies.

Sarah Stookey is a graduate student in the Department of Economics at the University of California, Riverside, and is a specialist on Nicaragua.

Clare Weber is a graduate student in Latin American Studies at California State University, Los Angeles.

Aníbal Yáñez is a participating editor of *Latin American Perspectives* and a doctoral candidate in Latin American Studies at the University of California, Berkeley.

Index